Built By
RESILIENCE

Built By
RESILIENCE

Turn Every
Setback
Into Your
Comeback

Shaina Zazzaro
Creator of the "One More Minute Rule"

INDIE BOOKS
INTERNATIONAL

Built By RESILIENCE

Turn Every Setback Into Your Comeback

© 2025 Shaina Zazzaro
All rights reserved.

Printed in the United States of America.

The One More Minute Rule™ is a trademark of Effortlessly Healthy.

Effortlessly Healthy® is a registered trademark of Effortlessly Healthy.

Disney® is a registered trademark of Disney Enterprises, Inc.

Little Debbie® is a registered trademark of McKee Food Corporation.

Starbucks® is a registered trademark of Starbucks Corporation.

MyFitnessPal® is a registered trademark of MyFitnessPal, Inc.

CrossFit® is a registered trademark of CrossFit, LLC.

Instagram® is a registered trademark of Instagram, LLC.

Google® is a registered trademark of Google LLC.

Dawn® is a registered trademark of The Procter & Gamble Company.

ISBN 13: 978-1-966168-32-4
Library of Congress Control Number: 2025920524

Designed by Melissa Farr, Back Porch Creative, LLC

INDIE BOOKS INTERNATIONAL®
2511 WOODLANDS WAY
OCEANSIDE, CA 92054
www.indiebooksintl.com

Table Of Contents

Preface   1

1   Why Resilience Will Change Your Life   5

2   Built By Resilience: My Story   17

3   Transform Your Self-Talk, Transform Your Life   29

4   Discover the Superpower Already Inside You   35

5   Your Health Is Your Greatest Wealth   43

6   The One More Minute Rule   53

7   Entrepreneurship: Surviving The Potholes   63

8   Success Is Never A Straight Line   71

9   Turn Every Setback Into A Comeback   79

10 Celebrate The Progress, Not Just The Goal   87

11 Perfectly Imperfect   97

12 Own Your Resilient Future   105

Appendix
A   *Acknowledgments*   *111*
B   *Big Four Shainaisms*   *115*
C   *About The Author*   *117*
D   *Works Cited And Author's Notes*   *119*

Preface

I used to believe in the power of manifestation. Believe you can, and you will achieve. Visualize your goals, and you will attain them. It was a wonderful concept, all wrapped up like a perfect gift. If you can believe it, you can manifest it.

Let's get real—that's not how life works.

Don't get me wrong—we all have within us the ability to create the future we want. But I will proudly tell you now that *manifestation* is not the goal.

When you embrace the concept of manifestation, two key things will happen in your life. First, you will be giving away your power to the universe, a higher being, fate, whatever you wish to call it.

Giving away your power means you no longer have control over the outcome. You cannot control what will happen, how it will happen, or when it will happen.

All the success that I have is because I put in the *hard work* and made it happen. I put into motion what transpired, and I worked to achieve the results I have.

Even Disney gets this concept right. In the movie *Aladdin*, Aladdin wants the princess. Yes, he finds a magic genie in a bottle, but guess what? He ends up losing that genie to the nemesis character.

The movie does not end there. Aladdin fights for the princess, utilizing his strength and the experiences he has had along the way to save her and trick the villain into self-banishment. (I don't want to give too much away.) In the end, the genie does not win the princess for Aladdin. Aladdin wins her over with himself.

By choosing manifestation, the second thing that happens in your life is that you are saying you are no longer responsible for your destiny. If you are no longer responsible, then you can easily just accept your fate as reality.

I am here to tell you, "No!" *Never settle*, especially if this is not the life you want or envisioned for yourself. Your life can be extraordinary!

Now, that doesn't mean that you won't have failures. I have had more failures and setbacks than I would even care to admit. But the funny thing about failures: They have led me to the amazing successes I now have.

I have failed up, and so can you.

My mom was a single mom, and she was the foundation that led me to develop my resilience. She was strong. She was brave. And she was always my reason for continually fighting for what I want. I grew up seeing her in and out of bad relationships. My sister, Nikki, ended up with the wrong crowd and her life was taken too soon. I decided I had a different path.

I made it my life goal to take care of my mother. I knew if she had me in her corner, she would never have an experience like those again. My entire life has been devoted to being able to take care of my mother and keep her safe.

Those early years taught me that resilience isn't just about bouncing back from setbacks. It's about recognizing that the small daily disappointments can accumulate and become overwhelming if you let them.

When my company faced countless minor challenges—equipment failures before major events, staff not showing up during our busiest times, or clients being clients—I drew on the same inner strength. I took one minute to regroup, remember my purpose, and put myself back into giving my all. Each small hurdle threatened to derail my momentum, but I reminded myself that the distance between where I stood and my goals only appeared vast because of how far I'd already climbed.

The business landscape often mirrored my personal life: unpredictable and requiring constant adaptation. Opportunity arrived not when I was actively searching for it, but when I was simply focused on keeping my business alive through unprecedented circumstances. Success, I've learned, rarely announces itself with fanfare—it often slips in through a side door you didn't even know was open.

What I know now is that the fire inside me was never extinguished by these setbacks because I refused to see them as endpoints. The path to success isn't a straight ascent but rather a series of plateaus, occasional backslides, and unexpected leaps forward.

The resilience I developed watching my mother, protecting my own dreams, and building a business despite countless small obstacles—this is the foundation where lasting success is built. It is not in avoiding the hurdles, but in developing the strength to keep climbing despite them.

This is the story of how a young girl, brought up with a single mother and a little sister, turned her roller-coaster life from nothing into something. This is a story of perseverance. This is a story of resilience.

This is *my* story.

I hope this book inspires you, a guide to living your best life, and the perseverance to overcome failure (and there will be plenty of it).

Keep pushing forward and embrace the failures. They will lead you to the success you want!

Mom's birthday, one of the last spent with Nicole.

1

Why Resilience
Will Change Your Life

My story could have been very different. From being raised by a single mom and living on an up-and-down financial roller coaster, there were countless times when I crumbled. I was, admittedly, a troubled kid. I could have used any of these excuses to take an easier and much less successful path.

Instead, I chose to take the hard route so that I could provide for my mom the way she provided for me.

For example, even though I had been skipping school, I refocused and graduated a year early from high school, then went on to college, only to drop out for a time (a story I will share with you later in the book).

Many of my choices were solid, and some were not. That is how life is. You cannot believe that all of your choices and all of life's circumstances will always provide a straight shot to success.

Believe me, there are curves and even sudden drops off a cliff. How you choose to take on things that happen will test your resolve.

I feel like now more than ever, if something happens to you, it's very easy for you to become the victim. My mom could have been the victim. I could have been the victim. Hell, I was the victim for a period of time.

It is up to you to choose how you define yourself. You are the only person in charge of your feelings. Learning how to overcome obstacles, especially things that could derail your progress, is a key attribute to success.

It's natural for people to hit low points. I cannot imagine how many low points my mom had as a single mother of two kids. She rarely showed any pain that she was experiencing when I was growing up—she kept calm and she persevered. That lady showed me strength, no matter what.

Humans have emotions, and it depends on how you learn to manage them and navigate through different situations. I'm not going to lie; this is easier said than done. I'll admit, there are times I have completely crumbled, but it is how you bring those pieces back together.

Here's the thing: When it comes to resilience, it's something that you have to channel from deep down inside of you, no matter how hard it is.

I always share in my keynotes about lighting a fire. There have been times in my life that were very difficult and, yes, I always did figure things out. But that doesn't mean I didn't want to give up or give in. I had to find the fire deep within and let it burn. Sometimes it was harder to start the fire than others, but no matter what, I made it happen. I would take one minute to rekindle that fire within.

Let's fast forward: After dropping out of college to take a call center job, going back, replacing F's with A's, and graduating summa cum laude, I thought I was going to land my dream job. Yet, I couldn't.

I had stopped my college education a week before the end of my last semester for my associate's degree. When I went back to school, I was an older student. I was the oldest one in my class, and I had to let go of judgment. I told myself, you can do it. I told myself I'd graduate and that I'd make it.

I got through college on food stamps, unemployment benefits, and credit card debt. It was so low for me because I had built myself up to have achieved so much more at this point. I went through many challenges. After graduation, I had to take a low-paying job to pay the bills and make ends meet.

My independence went into overdrive during these moments. In the back of my mind, my mother being a single mother of two was always there, and I wanted to save her. I pushed through my own fears to reach for the goal I had set for myself.

There was nothing more complex than the moment when I realized no matter what I believed, this dream didn't happen. So, now what? I had to find that fire inside of myself to say, OK, get it together, move on. You can do it. You can believe in yourself. Stay strong, figure it out—take the one minute to allow the pivot.

If I think about it in every situation ever, it's a mental muscle that I have developed. Resilience starts with your mind. You must constantly remind yourself that you can do something, because if you start to feel negative, you will quickly lose momentum.

If you're negative, you're not going to get past the current failure you are facing. And let's face it: When things are going well, you usually don't start to have negative thoughts. If you tell yourself that you can't do something, you're not going to do it.

Why do women in business in particular need to practice resilience? Many women that I know say that, as women in business, they are not seen or heard.

My advice is that you have to keep working to be seen and to have a voice. The fastest way to do that is to prove to people what you're capable of and that you are someone who should not be discounted. Don't keep living in fear of being seen. Get used to being loud and being heard. Exuding confidence—walking with your head held high and owning your worth is the straightest path.

I've dealt with a lot of people in business, including working with men. Many of them don't respect me as much as they do my husband. In those instances, I'll let it go while staying strong and choose a different path for the desired outcome. I will look for an opportunity where I can remind them that I'm the one who just signed that check. I'm the one who has been in charge the whole time. I'm the one who owns this company.

There's nothing wrong with assertiveness at the right moment when the receiving party is at a point to hear that message. There's no problem with telling someone what you're capable of. Make confidence your greatest asset.

When I worked in a hospital setting, where most administrators were women and most doctors were men, I had no problem telling the doctors I was great. I had no problem showing them every day what I was capable of. That has to come with and from confidence.

Many of you might not be confident enough right now. I would argue that it all starts with your health and wellness. The healthier you are, the happier you are, and the better you feel about yourself. The more you invest in yourself, the more confident you're going to be. Mental and physical health go hand in hand.

How Failures Build The Resilience Muscle

Failures feel awful in the moment, but they lead to success. The only way you fail is if you give up. There will always be situations where you feel that you are going to fail. That is when you need the resilience muscle to pivot and buy yourself more time to reach that success point. Everyone fails, but it's up to you to find your inner strength when it feels like the world is totally against you. Don't let the fear of failure dictate your success.

As many of you know, I started my first company in 2013 with a dollar and a dream. I have grown this business into a successful, multimillion-dollar company and achieved my dream of becoming a thirty-five-year-old millionaire. If only it were a clear shot to that success point, but it was not.

Within the first two years of my business, I had one hundred customers, and I felt great. I didn't realize at the time that I didn't have the right customer service platform in place. The quality of my product suffered, and I dropped down to seven customers. I had built up my company, only to fall way back. I had to figure out a way to turn that situation around.

The Four-Step Rule

From these and other experiences, I have created a four-step rule to get back into the game. It is simple yet effective for engaging (or reengaging) your perseverance muscle.

1 Feel The Emotions Of Loss   2 Assess Your Situation   3 Create A Plan   4 Take Action

Step One: Feel The Emotions Of Loss

You are not a robot. You are going to have days where you feel anxious, depressed, overwhelmed, sad, or just angry (or all of the above at the same time). All of those emotions are tied to loss.

Allow yourself to feel those emotions so you can move past them. You are only temporarily stuck, but it can feel like there is no end in sight. It is OK to feel anxious, depressed, overwhelmed, sad or just plain angry. I have dropped to the ground and cried. What matters more is what you do once this happens. Will you let the hardships and failures dictate your future or will you learn and get back up?

Give yourself one more minute to assess how you feel. Then get up, look at yourself in the mirror, and tell yourself you are in control of your life. If you do that, you are ready for the next step.

Step Two: Assess Your Situation

The fastest way to get out of a difficult situation is to stop, look around, and find an exit. Seems simple, right? Taking a moment to assess your situation will help you understand where you are and what went wrong.

You may know where you want to go, who you want to be, and what you want to do, but sometimes it is easier said than done. Take your moment to regroup, grab a pen and paper, write down a plan, and figure out the best way to go about it. If you have someone in your life who is bringing you down, remove them. If you are in a toxic environment at work, change it. Your life is your choice, and it is what you do with it that will dictate your future.

I explain to my chefs at my company that I look at every situation as a triangle. My goal is to get to the tip of the triangle. I can then look down and see processes, procedures, waste, and so on. If you aren't at the top, you cannot get the whole picture. And it takes just a minute to get there.

Step Three: Create A Plan

You know where you are, where you want to go, and what obstacles are in your way. Now, you can devise a detailed plan that takes into account your new situation. This is where mental agility comes in. How can you get out of this situation, and more importantly, who has the skill set to help? Addressing the community around you and sharing the plan focuses on communicating and being mentally prepared for feedback and even pushback, even if it's only for a minute.

Step Four: Take Action

Take action. This is the hardest part. So many people are afraid of failure that the thought of action is terrifying, but that is what will get you to where you want to be. That is what will make you shine, soar, life your best life. One small step can lead you to the right direction. No matter how hard it is, if you try, you are closer to getting to where you want to be, but if you never do, you'll never know.

You aren't in solitary confinement. You are not behind bars. You have the option to take action, so attack it head-on. That is a gift, to be able to fight another day, and it isn't one to waste.

How A Focus On Health Can Lead The Way To Wealth

I have struggled with my health over the course of my lifetime. I was overweight most of my life, the little overweight kid who was picked on. I was told I was fat and ugly, and I went home crying every day.

I love to eat. My grandfather would tell me during holidays to stop eating when I was on my third plate of food. I came from an Italian family. It didn't help that for several years we lived with my mom's fiancé and his three kids, and they were those genetically blessed kids who could eat whatever they wanted and not gain an ounce. And I would follow suit, but pay the consequences. Little Debbie was my girl. I also did very little physical activity.

During that time, we had a bunch of junk food in the cupboard. I would eat that junk food for hours like it was nothing. When I was in my early teens, I thought it was better for me to get a Frappuccino every morning than to eat breakfast. I didn't realize I was consuming nearly half of my daily calories in that one drink.

The most difficult thing was being picked on when I was growing up. I'll never forget fifth grade—the jerk who called me out on being a size sixteen. I had accidentally gone to school with new pants and left the size sticker on them. I went home, I cried, but I had no choice, I had to keep going back to school. I had to be strong, strong like my mom. I got used to it. I was the heavy kid, and I accepted that. I was fine until I turned twenty-one, and I was up to 195 pounds, the biggest I've ever been in my life. I went to a nightclub to apply for a bartender position.

I had taken a bartending course, so I knew what to do by the books, but I had no practical, real-life experience—it was a basic course where I learned how to make basic drinks. It didn't truly prepare me to go into the busiest nightclub in Rochester, New York.

But that was what I did. I told them I was a great bartender. The manager hired me and put me at the busiest bar on the first night, and I crushed it. I found out I was actually a great bartender. And it was a great confidence booster. I've never been afraid of hard work, and I always wanted to prove to people that I was the best if I said I was going to be.

And then another worker at the nightclub said the manager only hired me because he was a "chubby chaser." And I was like, "What does it even mean?" I had never even heard that term in my life. I had not been picked on since I was in eighth grade. And now I was getting picked on again.

I have always been very extreme. If I commit to a new venture, I go all in. As far as I was concerned, there's no point in going in half-assed with anything. At that moment, I decided to eat healthily and incorporate exercise into my daily routine. This was a turning point for me, pushing me to completely transform my lifestyle.

This journey has not been a straight line. I lost fifty pounds, and with each of my children, I gained it back. But I had the formula, and I knew I could be stronger than my past. Each time, I lost the weight again. Today, I am in the best health of my life and the strongest I have ever been. And I am just getting started.

Yes, it is easy to complain about life circumstances, but you, too, can be all in. You just have to decide that your past does not dictate your future.

It would have been very easy to stay comfortable as the overweight girl. Instead, I decided to write a different chapter for myself.

What chapter are you willing to rewrite?

One More Minute Rule

When you feel like you're falling apart, take one more minute to breathe, regroup, and remind yourself that resilience is built in moments just like this.

2

Built By Resilience: My Story

During my college years, I was diagnosed with severe psoriatic arthritis. I couldn't believe I had arthritis at such a young age. In my mind, that was something you developed when you got older. They put me on methotrexate, which is often used in conjunction with chemotherapy. I will never forget that week with methotrexate. I had to go to my grandparents' house, and I was in such bad shape that I needed them to take care of me. I slept on the couch for a whole week. It was bad.

I met with my physician, and I decided the methotrexate was not for me. He suggested that I join a phase III placebo-controlled clinical research study for a new medication. I've never felt so sick as I did that month I was on that new medication—it had gotten so bad that I underwent a colonoscopy at twenty-two years old. Since the research study was placebo-controlled, they could not tell me if I was still on the medication or not.

I decided to leave the study and instead clean up my diet. I met with a naturopathic physician in Arizona when visiting my mom, who had moved there just a few months prior. From that

17

initial appointment, I followed what the naturopath said for six months—I did not cheat at all. If a food item had more than three ingredients, I would not eat it. I was essentially on a very strict paleo diet. After six months, I went back to my rheumatologist, and he told me my disease was in remission.

I have not had a flare-up since I committed to healthy eating and have stuck with it. It made a huge difference.

This will be explored in future chapters, but I bring this up for a reason. A main part of your resilience story is your health. It is hard to be resilient if you are not prioritizing your health.

Notice I am not saying being completely healthy—your level of health may be very different from mine. When you invest in your body and mind, you are laying the foundation to build that resilience muscle.

Add movement, focus on eating healthily, and give yourself mental breaks—by doing this, you are giving yourself a fighting chance to improve your health. And with an improvement in your health, you can use that energy to deal with setbacks coming your way (because they are coming).

The other thing to remember is that your community can either lift you up or tear you down. Surround yourself with allies who truly have your back. My biggest ally is my husband, Mike.

Know Who Is In Your Corner

My husband, Mike, has always been ambitious. He graduated from high school in Spencerport, New York, and then studied at Johnson & Wales University to become a culinary master specializing in pastry. In fact, he was so ambitious that during his summers from college, he'd drive back home and run a hot dog cart, Zarro's.

Once he graduated from college, Mike began his culinary career as the opening pastry chef at Next Door Bar and Grill. He kept catering out of his mom's house when he wasn't working at a restaurant; he was working on trying to build his business. He started his food truck business, Chef's, in 2012, a year before I started my business. Mike always supported me. He taught me. He helped me, but he has never overstepped. I think the love story is an important part of the resilience story. He wasn't the hero who rescues the damsel in distress, but he became part of the team for my quest. I could go to him for advice. I mean, who else gets a culinary-trained chef as their unpaid consultant for starting their food delivery catering business?

I'll never forget it; it was the October food truck rodeo. The first time I caught a glimpse of his truck, I looked over. I thought to myself, "Who the hell's this guy in this Chef's truck?" Then, I didn't see him again until we were at an event, and he pulled up behind me. I was like, "It's the Chef's truck again."

I was so unprepared with my company; I didn't even have chalk for my board. I approached Mike and asked for chalk. Not only did he have some, but it was liquid chalk. Wow!

He then asked me if I'd like to see his high-end catering. I was floored. I went back to my food truck and told the woman working with me that I was going to make him fall in love with me and learn all of his tricks. He went back to his food truck, and the man working with him told him, "You are going to marry that girl." We have never missed a day talking after that, and we have been together twelve years.

Success Is Never A Straight Line

The first failure in my business was when I bought a 1978 Shasta RV, thinking it would work as a food truck, and then I realized that it was not going to function at all, and it was a bad move. I ended up selling it for parts to get more cash in. I had to figure out a way to get another loan to get another food truck.

Another failure that comes to mind after the Shasta was when I rented a warehouse and started building it out as a commercial kitchen. I realized I didn't have the money to keep going. During that time, I was also robbed. Someone smashed a brick through my window and took the little bit of money that I had from an event.

Life can throw a lot at you. I was on the verge of bankruptcy. At that moment, I had to choose to keep going. Believe me, throwing in the towel at that point would have been justified by so many people. Some even thought my decision to keep going was crazy, but I knew this was the right path. I just needed to figure out the pieces.

I had yet another setback when the guy who was the first chef working in my company, who was like a brother to me, ended up drinking a bit too much. We got in a fight one night while at a bar watching our favorite local band. He was *very drunk*. I told him to stop drinking since we had to go to a food truck event in the morning. I relied on him to drive the food truck. He hauled off and whacked me straight in the face! We were also roommates; we couldn't afford much when we started the company. I ended up kicking him out of the house.

Shortly after, I was unable to afford my rent and became homeless. I ended up having nowhere to live for a few months because I had no money to get my own apartment. I was floor surfing, slept in my car, and did what I had to do to survive. I didn't want to burden my family or let them know I was failing, so I worked to figure it out on my own.

It felt like everyone told me not to quit my steady job, and that starting a business was risky. Guess what? It is risky. In those moments, I could not let anyone know that I was failing. In order to achieve my destiny and dream, I had to be resilient and just keep going.

Seeing Red

When I was at that warehouse, I was grossing about $30,000 a month, and I thought it was fine. I had a few employees. I was able to get some help. But then, I started really getting into financial problems. Everything got expensive. I just didn't have the money.

I was down to negative bank accounts. I had submitted a bid to serve food at the CrossFit regional competition.

I called my mom for help. I begged her to move back to Rochester. She did it for me. She was finally living in Scottsdale, Arizona, her dream place, and came back for me. We still wince when we think about CrossFit Regionals. It was both a triumph and a trial. This was in my first year of business, and it was a trial by fire. It showed me what I was capable of and had me dig deep to find the strength to get through. And it helped me find that resilience muscle.

I never gave up—and CrossFit approved my bid at exactly the right time. One magical day, I got to the mailbox and there was a $23,000 check from CrossFit. I was able to pay my bills and do just enough to go to CrossFit regionals. I assembled a bunch of people for whom I barely had enough money to pay to work. I was able to borrow $5,000 for a refrigerated van. I found the only food distributor that I didn't owe money to and took out a $10,000 order. I packed everyone up. Then, we drove up to Cincinnati, Ohio, to serve in the middle of a college campus.

We ended up doing $40,000 of sales that weekend with no commissary and no real kitchen. I was waking up every three hours to run the food truck, ensuring the generator wouldn't die the next day. The event was so busy, we worked without stopping—we couldn't even go to the bathroom for hours!

I turned around and did that again two weeks later in Boston. These were two of the hardest weekends of my life. I would rather be in labor than do this ever again. That saved the business just enough to keep going just a little bit longer.

Still, I could not afford to build out that warehouse so it would pass the fire code inspection. I couldn't afford the hood and exhaust system. I found an inexpensive kitchen and moved my company to the local public market.

But then we reached a hundred customers. I was like, "OK, we're growing out of this space." I ended up finding a new kitchen to lease, but could not afford renovations. One of my old customers, who happened to be a master builder, was an angel and gave me a personal loan to do the build-out. He told me he didn't want anyone to take a percentage of what I built, and wanted to help. *Thank you, Gaetano.*

During this time, we kept our food truck in the parking lot of my one-bedroom apartment that I shared with my mom. We couldn't keep up. The truck didn't even have an oven. Why did I think I could do this? The quality went down and we dropped to having only a few customers, and we were screwed again. I thought everything was looking up, and then we just plummeted. Again.

I always kept failing, then figuring it out, and failing again, and then figuring it out.

Falling Into A Black Hole

From 2019 to 2024, I have seen amazing growth. I transformed my meal delivery, catering, and food truck business, Effortlessly Healthy, into a thriving, multimillion-dollar business, and was named #62 of the top 100 fastest growing companies and the #8 fastest growing MWBE (minority and women-owned business enterprise) by the Greater Rochester Chamber of Commerce (one of my many goals realized). Not only did I reach a business goal, but I reached a life goal—I turned myself into a self-made thirty-five-year-old multimillionaire.

You know what happens when you reach goals? You can't mess up. I know that there will be many hardships along the way, but it is up to me to figure them out and to be resilient. *Lack of resilience will lead to extreme failure.*

Lack of resilience will lead to extreme failure.

Pulling Yourself Out And Up

There have been times when I turned to the wrong things to manage my stress. I can reflect now and share that there were events with my food truck where I became completely drunk in order to survive the day and the pressure. I thought pinot grigio was my best friend.

There was even a time when I was so hammered, I accidentally threw out $2,000 in cash proceeds from a food truck event. I ended up having to dumpster dive to find the bag of cash I had tossed into the garbage.

We all know holes are bad, but how often do we fall into them, or even throw ourselves into them? I could have easily stayed in that hole, using alcohol or food as a way to cope.

At the end of the day, I had to be the one who decided that hole wasn't for me. I have asked myself this countless times before, and now I am asking you: Are you focusing on what you can control or what is beyond your control?

Failure and failings give you new information to learn and grow. And with failure can come people who have no problem kicking you when you are down.

When You Are Down, You Can Be A Target

I can clearly remember one food truck event. There were twelve food trucks with about six thousand people in attendance, so everyone was set to do well. My sister was supposed to show up to help me, as I knew we would be slammed.

I also had a lot riding on this event from a revenue standpoint. At that time in my life, I was essentially homeless. I was couch surfing, sleeping where anyone would offer me a place to crash for a few nights. I was trying to pull myself out of this financial pit and find a permanent roof over my head.

It was thirty minutes before the start of the event, and my sister was a no-show. I started crying in my food truck, with the waves of fear, grief, and disappointment crashing on me. One of the other food truck owners came over, in what I thought was an act of compassion.

What she was really doing was getting the scoop so she could go around to the other food truck owners and tell them how crazy I was. She had no idea the failures and stresses I was dealing with at that moment. And what was more, she didn't care.

Luckily, as the day started, someone I knew came over to order and could see my stress and panic. In a wonderful moment of community, he came into the food truck and started helping me cook and serve food. I also ended up crashing at his place for a couple of weeks after that—shout-out to him for helping me when no one else would.

Success is never a straight line. It is a roller coaster, and it is a crazy ride. You will always experience ups and downs. That is the whole point of life and life experiences. Never having failures can equate to living a smaller life—I didn't want that for myself, and I don't want that for you.

How others treat you can often be a reflection of how you treat yourself. It is very easy to let self-doubt and negative thoughts crowd your mind and drown out the confidence that is necessary to find that resilience muscle and start to work it. But how do you quiet down those negative voices?

Applying The Shaina Rule

Don't ever kick someone when they are down to make yourself feel bigger. You have no idea what someone else might be going through at that very moment. It takes a lot more effort to help someone and pick them up rather than hold them down. Be warned, however: The universe has a funny way of balancing things out.

One More Minute Rule

Before you talk yourself out of your big idea, spend one more minute imagining what's possible if it works.

3

Transform Your Self-Talk, Transform Your Life

*E*veryone self-talks, but people typically don't notice or admit that they self-talk. If you think about it, you probably talk to yourself multiple times a day. From the second you wake up, you tell yourself that you're going to get up. You're going to brush your teeth, you're going to check your cell phone—whatever you normally do.

The problem with self-talk is that a lot of people will tell themselves negative stuff more than positive. Think about when you're at work; your boss may tell you all the things you've done wrong. How many times does your boss actually tell you all the things you've done right? It's the same thing with yourself. A lot of people have a hard time looking at themselves and giving themselves some form of positive reinforcement.

I know it sounds silly, but there have been times when I look at myself in the mirror, and I'll either tell myself, "You look great," or "You don't look great." And believe me, I can be my own worst critic. However, I have also used self-talk to de-escalate a situation.

I've talked myself down from full-blown panic attacks. Just before one of my work trips, I had tape-in hair extensions for the first time—I had them for a photo shoot. And I thought, this looks great. I'm going to keep these in.

Fun fact about me: I struggle with anxiety—badly. Also, I don't like small spaces or the feeling of something around my head or stuck on me. I could feel the extensions on my head, and I knew that I would not be able to get them off easily.

I started thinking, "Oh my God. I can't do this." I was really starting to freak out. I looked in the mirror and said, "You look great. Keep them in." I talked to myself and talked myself down.

Second day, I went to bed. I couldn't fall asleep. It was one in the morning. I went to the bathroom; I looked in the mirror and I started telling myself, "Shaina, get it together. You are not going to let these hair extensions ruin your life."

At the same time, I was also thinking, "Do I have to get oil to get them out?" My mind wanted me to freak out, but I had to choose and get it together. I talked myself out of a full-blown panic attack over some tape-in hair extensions.

I realized the importance of being able to look myself in the eye while I self-talk. If you can't look in the mirror and say, "Don't have your panic attack," or "You look great today," no one else is going to be able to tell you that. You have to talk to yourself. Even at the gym, when I do bodybuilding, I realize it's so hard. I keep telling myself to "just do it." I look in the mirror and remind myself that I have to push through.

When the trainer's watching you, or your friend is over there lifting more weight than you, you have to keep going. This is true for everything. Even when I go out to eat, I find myself craving dessert all the time. You have to tell yourself that you can't eat the dessert. You have a choice, and you have to make that choice every time. Using self-talk can help you make the right choice at that moment.

In every single situation in life, you should either talk yourself out of a bad situation or build yourself up. It's when you start telling yourself, "I'm ugly, I'm fat, I'm stupid," that the negative things will start to destroy you. Everything starts with the way you talk to yourself. I always remind my kids that they are beautiful, kind, smart, brave, and funny. I want them to hear those words and repeat them.

There have been situations where my self-talk had to pull off a miracle. And practicing positive self-talk has kept me going. I share this story about the hair extensions that almost took over my mind in my keynotes. I refer to it often because of the amount of self-talk I had to do each day to handle something seemingly so small. It serves as a reminder that self-talk has shaped my future into what it is today.

My Bang Bang Shrimp Story

After I graduated summa cum laude from college, I felt certain I would land an amazing job in medical sales. I was young, smart, confident, and determined. I applied for job after job, and I got nothing, not even a call back.

I again was running out of money, and my plans had gone to the wayside. I ended up getting the only job I could—a waitress selling $5 "bang bang shrimp" (which are basically shrimp tossed in mayonnaise and sriracha).

Many families would come in and order this dish with water, so the bill could be as little as $10, and I would get a $1 tip. And I covered the lunch hour during the week—the worst shift imaginable. This felt like a fall from grace and a far cry from where I had been and where I had envisioned myself to be.

I also had to wear a fake chef's coat while selling this item. Instead of getting upset and allowing the negative feelings to take over, I decided to work on what I could control.

When I went to work, I made sure my chef's coat was immaculate. I made sure my hair and makeup were perfect, and my pants were clean and ironed. I also had my résumé ready to go, in case there was an opportunity.

Each day I went into work, I would introduce myself and say that I graduated summa cum laude with my degree and I was looking for a permanent job in the medical field. And I did this day after day after day.

My efforts finally paid off. I was covering for another waitress in a section I normally did not get. I was well-presented, and I had my introduction ready to go. I went over to this table and introduced myself and my backstory. This time, the audience was a perfect match. I was serving the CFO of one of the largest hospitals in the area.

He must have seen something, because he told me that he wanted to help and open a door that had been closed to me. He introduced me to a few departments that needed help from someone with my degree, and from that moment, I was able to secure two interviews and took a job that set me on the path to healthy eating and ultimately led to the creation of my company.

I could have sat there and kept being miserable and not communicating. I was so low that I temporarily stopped talking to myself. But I had to tell myself to get it together.

Each day I put on that chef's coat, I had to start over and tell myself that today could be the day I found the open door. Each day, I had to remind myself to be presentable and maintain a good attitude, because I didn't know who I would meet that day.

Self-talk is the first line of defense to getting you out of your own head and back in the game. If I had focused on what I hadn't accomplished at that point, that wonderful opportunity would have been missed.

That one opportunity not only led me to that amazing job and further confidence in my abilities, it also led me to create my organization. Those connections made my company grow to the powerhouse it is today.

One moment can change the course of your history. And one chat with yourself can set you up for the success you have always wanted. In each failure, all it takes is one small step to get momentum to get back on track. That momentum is already within you—you just need to find the way to let it out.

Applying The Shaina Rule

There is enough negativity in the world today. You don't need to add to it by telling yourself negative things. Instead, say that "You've got this," or "You will have a great day today." Take those ten seconds each morning and show some self-love with positive self-talk. Gratitude is everything.

One More Minute Rule

In your lowest moment, give yourself one more minute to believe you're still meant for more—because you are.

4

Discover the Superpower Already Inside You

Quit talking about manifesting.

My whole life, after reading the book *The Secret* by author Rhonda Byrne, I thought that I was manifesting everything.[1] I can't tell you how many times I have told my best friend how powerful I was—that I manifested something. I would say I wished it. It could be anything from getting a meeting on the books to predicting that an employee would not last a day in my company. Or it could be being able to manifest the power to believe in yourself enough to start a multimillion-dollar company, no matter how many times you fail.

And then I realized that I wasn't manifesting anything. It was all me. It was all because I told myself, and I found the fire in myself. Through my failures, I found my superpower. I believe that I am powerful enough to succeed in anything I do.

Self-Talk Revisited

Going back to the self-talk for a second, I can tell myself I'm capable of doing something. It is not a manifestation. There is no genie. I am making something happen. You take your desires, and you put them out into the universe. You believe that you are truly going to obtain them, and then here is the secret sauce: You make yourself obtain them. It's up to you.

It's not some magical manifestation. And it all ties in with self-talk. If I wake up saying, "I'm going to have a bad day," then I'm going to have a bad day. I could then use every instance that something goes wrong to think, "Oh my God, woe is me." If that is your attitude when your feet hit the floor, of course, you're going to have a bad day.

But if you have good intentions and tell yourself you're going to have a great day, you put a plan into action for your day. You end up doing whatever you want. It's all up to you to manifest your destiny. At the end of each day, every night, I will say I'm grateful for my friends, my family, my children, and my life. I am happy. I am healthy. My family is happy and healthy. That is putting good energy back out there.

I don't care what religion you are. It doesn't matter if you're talking to Jesus or if you're talking to God, or if you're just talking to something, you have to put those words out there. I would argue that if someone is looking at this from a religious angle, they are also talking to themselves and making it happen. It gives them some sort of faith. *The most important faith is the one you have in yourself.*

What Programming Are You Doing To Yourself?

Some people say you're programming your brain. Your brain is like a computer. What you're putting in there—the quality of the inputs into the computer—is going to be the quality of the outputs. Does that resonate with you?

If you're negative, you're going to be negative, and negative things will happen. If you're positive, you're going to be positive and do positive things. The same thing happens with the programming part of speech.

I tell my clients how important it is to have a schedule and to be consistent. And some of the things that I might say seem so simple, but they're not. Not everyone is doing everything they can to make an impact.

For example, your body is programmed to eat. It gets used to eating at certain times. It gets used to waking up at certain times. Many people wake up without an alarm. They're used to waking up every single day at a certain time. It's all about consistency in programming yourself.

Your body's like a computer. If you educate it, you give it healthy food, you provide it with exercise, you put everything into it, you will get great results. If you tell yourself that you can't do something, if you sit on your ass and just eat junk food all day, if you don't exercise, if you don't move, if you have no sort of structure, you're going to have an unstructured life.

It's up to you to create your life based on your habits. It all starts with your habits that come from your self-talk.

Your superpower comprises the habits you create to move toward your goal. Without them, you will be aimlessly wandering, hoping for the best.

Seeing The Superpower In Others

Several years ago, a very close friend reached out to me; she was struggling with an addiction, but had gotten herself clean. She liked the culture at Effortlessly Healthy and knew that it would be a supportive environment for her.

She had known me when we were younger and had always thought that I was mean. She started working with me and quickly realized I was not the horrible young girl she thought I was. She ended up showing me a letter that she wrote for herself, right before she started working for me. It said, "In a year, I want you to have a good job. I want you to break out of your addiction. I want you to feel fulfilled. I want you to have $X, Y,$ and Z in life."

And a year later, she again shared the letter with me, "Shaina, look what I found. This was because of you. You believed in me enough. You told me that I was capable, and I did it, and I have literally gotten my dream life because of you."

That is the nicest thing anyone has ever said to me. I pushed this woman so much because I saw what she was capable of. She didn't see that she could run my company. However, I saw the fire in this woman that she didn't see in herself.

It took her until she had worked with me for three years, and we had experienced some operations and HR turnover, for me to say, "Are you ready yet?"

And she finally said, "I am." And now this woman is running my company, and I trust her completely.

One of my greatest pleasures is speaking and volunteering with the Rochester Junior Achievement Academy. I spoke to a group of eighty young women recently, sharing with them my *Built By Resilience* keynote. Several of the ladies came up to me after my speech. They shared that they were ready to give up and my speech inspired them to keep going. I provided those ladies with the opportunity to apply for one of my scholarships.

Several of the young women in attendance, when applying for one of the scholarships, shared in their application that they were impressed with my vulnerability when I shared my struggles and hardships. Because of this vulnerability, they were moved to share theirs and be confident in sharing their stories.

Letting Your Superpower Shine

I remember the first time that I spoke in front of an audience. It was during college, and I took a public speaking class. I got straight A's for the class, but there was something more that happened.

Even when I stood up in class to speak, I was never nervous. I talked about things from the heart, and I was not worried about being judged. This was largely due to the fact that, as I looked out into the classroom, I saw many students who were nervous, and many of them had yet to present. I had a secret tip: when you speak, find a couple people who are interested in what you are saying and talk directly to those people. The whole room will think you are looking at everyone as you move between those individuals.

Fast forward to 2023, when I started with my personal trainer, I noticed he was putting himself on social media quite a bit. I had been on live TV, which was different in my mind. The people who are interviewing you and watching are already interested in you. They know what they want to talk to you about.

When I first started posting on Instagram, sharing videos of myself making a recipe or sharing information, I felt incredibly exposed. It made me more nervous than being on live television! When you are on social media, you are in a vulnerable state. TV is a professional interview, where they are talking to Shaina, the CEO of the company.

When posting personal things, it is very raw. That puts you into a state where people can judge you. They may not know that I am a CEO—that shield gets removed—they only see Shaina. I am no one to them at that point.

I had even tried dying my hair blonde to be more "relatable," and I ended up getting back to my natural brunette hair color. Instead of trying to fit into someone else's ideal, I decided to embrace my own.

I also saw that with the confidence I found by being more natural and being more human, my TV interviews became more natural. I do have to remind myself, even today, that I am a different person. No one is judging me for being the overweight bartender. No one is judging that I have an ugly outfit on. It shows the overall confidence I have in my skin and being attuned to my superpower.

What is your superpower? What can you do that sets you apart, even just in your head, that can add to your confidence?

Find That Voice

One of my closest friends will share her opinion with me, and it is an opinion I trust. She has overcome so much and has found her path to success. I sent her my speeches and later called her, and she said, "I just wanted to say thanks."

She said, "You inspired me, and no one inspires me. I should be thanking you, Shaina."

I said, "Well, what did I do?"

She said, "I listened to your speech, and let me tell you, I was tired. And man, I didn't want to do anything. I was lying on the couch all day."

Her boyfriend had come home with fast food for lunch.

She said, "I ate some garbage lunch, and then I just felt awful. And I just lay there. As I was lying there, I was listening to your speeches, and I said, 'Shaina Zazzaro told me to get up.' You told me to get up, and now I am living the rest of my day. I'm not lying around. And I'm not eating junk food for dinner. I'm having a salad, and I feel great."

And even though I have heard that over and over, I am still elated that it works, because it does!

Someone needs to tell you: get up, move. That someone can be me, and then I want you to transfer that someone to you. You can start telling yourself, "Go for a quick walk, make a healthier lunch, put in the extra few minutes on that job assignment to make it stellar."

It all starts and ends in your head. Don't wait for some manifestation genie to show up and give you the success you want. Take one step to create that future reality right now.

Applying The Shaina Rule

Stop giving away your power to someone or something to grant your wishes. You will be waiting forever with nothing to show for it. You have a set time on this earth. Each moment is meant to create something amazing. Take one action today, whether it is eating something healthier, taking a walk to help reduce your stress, connecting with a loved one, trying something you have been putting off, anything really! Today is your day to have a great day.

One More Minute Rule

When you want to quit on your purpose,
spend one more minute remembering
who you're doing it for.

5

Your Health Is Your Greatest Wealth

The most important rule to remember is this: you have to take care of yourself. The number one thing I've realized is that you feel better when you look better. You have to have proper hygiene. That's one thing that most people might not think about. Proper hygiene includes brushing your hair, brushing your teeth, showering, creating healthy eating habits, figuring out what exercises you enjoy doing, doing them enough, and enjoying them enough to make them consistent habits.

Creating habits that benefit your body, mind, and overall well-being is the cornerstone of achieving success. I have a lot of people who are Effortlessly Healthy clients who email me saying they want to lose weight. The first thing I tell them is if you want to lose weight—and you can do this for any goal in your life— write down for a week what you're eating. Write down what your habits are. Consistency is key and the only want to achieve goals.

Know Your Habits To Change Them

I recommend MyFitnessPal.[2] Record your food and be honest. Don't lie about it. If you eat the doughnut, put the doughnut in. I'm not going to judge you. But in order to change a habit, you have to see what your habits are first.

A lot of people just get so used to doing the same things. They don't even realize that there's something they should change. My friend Lisa and I were talking, and she said, "I noticed I was going to the grocery store at a certain time. At first, I got a doughnut beforehand because I was hungry. The next thing I knew, I was always getting a doughnut and coffee before I went to the grocery store. I ended up changing the time that I would go to the grocery store (to right after breakfast) so I would not be tempted to stop and get the doughnut.

"Once I acknowledged that I was always getting the doughnut and the coffee, I started eating a healthy breakfast and then going to the grocery store. That one change moved the needle and helped me to get my weight back down."

It's little changes like that that can make your life better, and it is true for everything. It's mental. It's physical. And health starts with healthy eating. I don't care what anyone says. Healthy eating is 90 percent of being healthy. It doesn't matter if you're a bodybuilder like me and you're working out an hour and a half a day: You can't out-train a bad diet.

I could work out until I'm blue in the face. I cannot have junk food. If I trained the way I do and then I went and had dessert every single day, I wouldn't see any results.

How I Leveled Up

I have achieved a sixty-plus-pound loss following the birth of my second child, Michael, and forty of those pounds were just from walking. I had my son in September 2019, right before COVID-19. We had nothing to do besides walking. I bought this amazing stroller. I found a trail, and we would go walking every day. If we didn't go to the trail to walk, I found a three-mile path near my house.

I would go outside and walk. It kept my kids busy. It got me out. I liked it, and it helped me lose weight in conjunction with healthy eating. The walk would also help to take my mind off things, almost like a meditation exercise. That hour gave me a physical and mental break. I got to the point where I'm doing the Peloton, and walking, walking, walking. I walked so much on a treadmill that I injured my knee and ended up in a knee brace and needing knee surgery a few years later.

I realized I needed to take things up a notch. I was going to this gym, and I saw a woman that I had tended bar with back at a nightclub. I said, "What are you doing? How do you know how to lift weights?"

She replied, "You have to lift weights. This is what's going to take you from where you are to where you want to be: weight training. Find Ivan."

I feel like everyone always has this common misconception of weight training: That somehow, they are going to look like a giant, jacked bodybuilder. That's not it. If you see the most toned people, they strength train. Strength training is important, especially as we age. The older you get, the more muscle you will lose. The way to bring the muscle back is through strength training.

I found Ivan. When I first met Ivan, my trainer, I told him I wanted to train with him five days a week. If I start something, I will go all in. I'm not going to half-ass anything.

He'd probably heard that a million times. He said that I could come in and do a trial day with him. I arrived at 8:00 a.m. the next day, and in the gym, I saw these women whose bodies I couldn't believe were that strong.

When I was working out on my first day, I thought there was no way I could get bodies like some of these women. They were jacked. Ivan started having me lift weights, and I had to push through the self-talk and get back to a strong mental state.

Those first couple of weeks were tough—some of the hardest stuff I've ever done. I couldn't sit on the toilet without pain. Imagine going to the bathroom, and you are physically in so much pain just to sit down that you feel like you can't stand up to get off the toilet. It hurt so bad. But I didn't stop. I had to tell myself, "You want this, and you need to go for it."

Even recently, I had knee surgery, which I had put off for years. One of the hardest things was the fact that I had to stop moving to let my knee heal. And when I was able to get moving again, I slept better and I felt better. Movement is life, and we are designed to move. I took physical therapy very seriously so I could get back in the gym. I combined that with healthy eating and muscle building to speed up my recovery.

My Weak Moment

In conjunction with Effortlessly Healthy, where I have access to healthy meals and my trainers, I have stayed consistent.

Now, I have always had the goal of getting a flat stomach. I was always convinced that because I was a heavy kid growing up, my stomach was stretched out. When I got pregnant, I was a big girl. I ate a lot of food. I always thought, "OK, you have excess skin there."

Ivan told me, "Nope, that's fat. That's not skin. Keep going."

I was six months into my workout regimen with my trainer. I was working out harder than I've ever worked out in my life. I was eating healthfully, yet I gained a couple of pounds. And I got really pissed off at myself, so I called the plastic surgeon. I told him, "I'd like a tummy tuck."

I told the doctor during the consultation, "I've lost fifty pounds three times. I need a tummy tuck. I want to get this over with. I'll pay for the surgery. Can you explain the process to me?"

The doctor then explained the procedure. "First, I am going to start by cutting your stomach at the top, and pull your stomach up. So, your belly button and everything will be flat. Then, I need to cut off that excess skin, and I will staple the incision shut. You will then be bandaged up, and you're going to have drainage bags on the side. The procedure will cause you to be bent over for a week or two. But it's very easy healing."

And I'm like, "That is what you consider easy healing?" I went back to Ivan and told him, "I called about a tummy tuck."

He said, "Just stick to the plan. Be consistent. You're not being consistent enough. If you want it, don't deviate from the plan. Just stay consistent."

So, I stayed consistent. It took several more months, and I got my flat stomach. It's not that perfect six pack, but it's enough for me to be happy without going under the knife. My son reminds me of it frequently and counts my abs. Every year, I know I'm going to get better because I achieved a goal that I could visually see. And I did for myself, which is important.

Being OK With Not Being OK

You are never going to be 100 percent at the top of your game 100 percent of the time. That is not sustainable. Life will sometimes knock you completely down. In those moments, you need to be OK with not being OK.

When I was pregnant with my daughter, we had recently moved our kitchen to a bigger place on South Avenue. I can picture the location as if I visited it yesterday. My mom was helping me plate food for delivery.

Something set me off, and with the stress of the move, the stress of being pregnant, the stress of wanting my business to succeed, I lost it—and I lost it big time. I started destroying every single plate of food on the table.

I had tried to act as if everything was OK, and the pressure had to go somewhere, and somewhere it did. After this explosion, I walked over to my doctor's office and told her that I needed help.

Even today, my mind can get totally fried. When you recognize that you are getting overworked, overwhelmed, or just over it, stop what you are doing. Be a little bit selfish and take a day or even a few days to reset and recalibrate. It is OK to admit you are mentally fried and acknowledge that you are stressed out and that you need a break. Sometimes, just letting your employees or community know that you are not 100 percent there can get you the support you need.

Don't feel for one second that you need to always "have it together." It is OK to heal anxiety to the best of your ability with mental and physical activities to reduce stress and provide that release.

If you don't give yourself a stress-release opportunity, your mind will choose one. And believe me, it will be at the worst time and place for that to happen. Step back, walk away, and put yourself back together. It is better to admit you need a break, to admit you need help, than to hurt others around you.

Step back, walk away, and put yourself back together.

Setting Goals Just For You

It's important that you have goals for yourself. So many times, people do things for everyone else. Take my company's success, for example. I wanted to be successful because I wanted to take care of my mom and my kids.

Weightlifting, one could argue, is incredibly selfish. I go to the gym every morning. My mom comes to my house to babysit my kids so I can get my hour and a half to myself at the gym.

I schedule every meeting in my life around my gym schedule, which is, for me, my time for stress and anxiety relief. I told my employees that my gym schedule is critical for my mental health.

And I did it for myself. I have struggled with anxiety my whole life. The exercising that is part of my daily habits helps me mentally, as well as physically. Even if you're feeling stressed out or tired, if you get up and take a walk, you're going to feel better. You're going to get more energy, and you will start to improve your health.

It is OK to prioritize your health, both physical and mental. If you are not healthy, you cannot support anyone else. We seem to be a society that frowns upon someone prioritizing themselves. I want to tell you that it is OK to do that—take care of yourself first, then you can take care of loved ones around you.

Applying The Shaina Rule

You can't out-train a bad diet. What you put into your body affects everything about your health, including weight, stress, illness, and fatigue.

It is imperative that you incorporate healthy habits and goals into your life that are just for you. Make health and wellness a priority—read labels, eat healthy foods, learn portion control, and enjoy movement. Find a sport or workout that you enjoy, and learn to love it. You will feel better and live longer if you take care of yourself. You cannot take care of others if you do not take care of yourself.

One More Minute Rule

Before you throw in the towel, give yourself one more minute to ask: "What if this setback is actually a shift?"

6

The One More Minute Rule

There were days I didn't think I'd make it.

Not metaphorically—literally. I was sleeping in my car, alone, trying to keep a brand-new business alive with nothing but a dollar and a dream. I had no home, no backup plan, and no time to fall apart. My life felt like it was crumbling, and I was trying to pretend I still had control.

One night, after a twenty-hour day of deliveries, no sleep, and no sign that anything was working, I looked at myself in the mirror of my rearview and whispered:

"Just one more minute, Shaina."

Not just one more day—that was too far away. Not just one more hour—I didn't have the strength. Just one more minute.

To hold it together. To take a breath. To not give up.

I didn't know it at the time, but that tiny moment became my anchor. It became a mantra. It became my resilience reset.

What Is The One More Minute Rule?

It's simple: You don't have to be strong forever. Just give yourself one more minute.

One more minute of courage. One more minute of effort. One more minute of belief when everything feels impossible.

It's what I used to survive being homeless. It's what I used to climb out of near-bankruptcy. It's how I rebuilt my body, my mind, and my confidence after trauma and grief. And it's how I've stood on stage—shaking, judged, vulnerable—and still stood tall.

The Minute That Changes Everything

Resilience doesn't always roar. Sometimes, it whispers: "Just one more minute."

That's the minute you don't give up. The minute you keep going. The minute that separates who you were from who you're about to become.

So the next time life hits you hard, don't try to fix the whole thing. Just give yourself one more minute. That's all it takes to start a comeback.

Habits That Stick In That One Minute

I may sound like a broken record, but habits can keep you on track, especially when you have a slip or a failure, which happens to all of us. And there are things you can do to keep that forward momentum, even when you feel like you are slipping back. You are human – remember that.

Get yourself on a schedule, and tell yourself you can do it. Get up and work out. Find a friend who can take a walk with you. Go outside and move. Drink water instead of soda. Those habits cost nothing.

There are many other things that you can do to consistently get to the point of success. And your path is going to be personal to you. Several years ago, I was heavy. People now see the woman I am right now. I have to remind them I was heavy by posting my heavy pictures to show a transformation, because it's part of my journey. I didn't magically become thin. I consistently and slowly ate healthfully and exercised to create this healthy lifestyle. I didn't get the quick fix, and I didn't get that tummy tuck. I listened when I was told that I didn't need it. I toughed it out and waited.

I don't have a flat stomach like that tummy tuck would've given me. My stomach is not super flat. And I am OK with that. That showed me that I was consistent, and I did it naturally on my own. And that's a good feeling. It's a good feeling when you can look in the mirror and say, "You did it. No matter how long it took you to get there, you didn't take the easy way out."

Taking Back Your Power

I was always looked at as the underdog. I remember when I was an intern. I was in a meeting with an executive who told me to get a master's degree in order to get to the level of success I have now.

While he thought he was giving me sound advice, I decided instead to take a different tactic. Honestly, I was not sure I would stay in hospital administration, and while earning a master's degree was certainly something that I could do, my intuition told me something else.

Because of the path I took to get to that job, I knew I wanted to do well. However, I never went in with the idea that I needed to impress my boss. I was looking to use my degree and become the best administrator they've ever seen. I focused on the job at hand. In my mind, my efforts had to pay off.

When people start their careers, they forget that they learned to study and work hard. In school, every assignment comes with a grade. I looked at this job as another class and each task as an assignment.

I looked at this job as another class
and each task as an assignment.

I wanted to get an A+ in every assignment. And I knew that every assignment was critical to get that A+ grade. Thinking that something is beneath you is a limiting thing to think, because it makes you believe that there isn't an opportunity to learn in every assignment.

One of my first tasks given to me at the hospital was horrible. I had to visit every office in the department of surgery and ensure that each computer had a barcode. It was mundane work that didn't align with my degree, but that didn't matter. I not only made sure each computer had a barcode, but I also tracked each barcode number to each office.

In my next assignment, I was given a box of keys that had probably been in the making for five years. I had to figure out the lock for each key. I had an intern at the time to help me sort the keys. This also gave me a taste of working with a team on something that feels like a waste of time, but is critical to someone. We worked together and figured out every single key in that box.

Nothing is beneath you on the road to success. You never know what leads to the next big opportunity, and what skills you will pick up along the way. Always give 110 percent. Because people may not remember the task you did, but they will certainly remember the attitude that came with it.

I also look at how you carry yourself in public. No matter what, you have to keep in mind your behavior in public. You are judged by your first interaction. I tell my kids this daily.

I was at Starbucks, and as I was chatting with the barista, the customer next to me recognized my voice from TV. He then said his neighbor receives my Effortlessly Healthy meals and has for the past ten years, and raves about the meals. Amazing.

What if I was having a bad day and instead of remaining calm, I was rude in the Starbucks instead? What would that ripple effect have been? Would he have recognized my voice, made the connection, and then gone home and said something to his neighbor? Would that person have decided to stop being a loyal customer? You never know who might be listening.

The real world provides the real tests. When I was in school, I never understood the value of working within a team. Anytime I had a group assignment, I got annoyed. Not surprisingly, in those assignments, I was the leader and did the most work. Anyone who was in my group knew they were going to get an A.

I was good at these assignments because I understood how to leverage resources available, like the library and the teaching assistant. For the first few years of my business, I had only myself and my mom. I could not offer any money to get the help I needed. We had to work as a team and remember we had each other. As the main staff, when we acquired some customers, we were able to hire staff part time and we were the ones working twenty-plus hours a day. We were able to do that because we had a goal to work toward.

My mom is the kind of person who does things on her own. I would have a hard time keeping employees when my mom was managing them, only because she would do all the work on her own and then feel like she was overworked.

I put the correct people in the correct positions with my team. They are working together as a team to make the company work, and work well. Instead of getting B's and C's, my team is focused on getting A's now. And I am more appreciative of having a stellar team, like a professor feels with amazing students in the class.

Being successful in life means working together. You cannot worry just about yourself. This also makes a difference in your happiness. I now love having a team with awesome people working under me.

I still have to fight against preconceived notions about me. People still look at me as a young, pretty female, and I am still asked if I make my food by myself in my kitchen at home. I am happy to report that I have a team of four professional chefs in a state-of-the-art facility. And knowing I have that team is one of the best ways to let go of those comments.

Manifesting is setting the goal that you want—it doesn't get you to achieve the goal. And when you set up that course for success, you have to be ready to take a leap of faith and put in the time and effort to get there. Yes, it will mean being exhausted, and that is just temporary. Anything worth doing is worth doing well.

Manifestation Takes More Than A Minute

Somehow, I will think of success, and it will suddenly be there with little to no effort from me.

No.

If you want that successful career, that financial freedom, and a healthy body and mind, you have to put in the work to get there. We are constantly looking for easy ways to succeed, and that starts early with us.

America lives in a fast-food world, and people don't even realize that that's a quick fix. You are going to take out instead of just making yourself food. If you need help with time or knowing how to prepare something healthy, invest in meal prep for a month and see how that affects your health. Preparing meals at home is an investment in your diet, as it teaches you to portion control and choose healthy options. Meal kits are a way to start learning those habits.

On the business side, I could have purchased a prospect list or bought followers on Instagram, rather than building relationships and a customer base. The same concept applies in both business and health; quick fixes are tempting. There are a lot of people who make a lot of money selling quick fixes.

There are so many false promises or costs associated with these shortcuts. But one thing is always universal: If you want continued success, you have to do the work. There's no promise that can create success more than actually working for it.

I think about my company's successes and failures, and whether there could have been quick fixes to get me to this point of sustainable success. There were none. I busted my ass every second of every day to get to this point. It's been hard, yet the level of success has been worth it.

I busted my ass every second
of every day
to get to this point.

The consistent actions you take in your life every day are what will get you where you want to go. It is what you do every day that counts toward that goal line.

Applying The Shaina Rule

The temptation to take a shortcut is around every corner. By staying the course and putting in consistent work, you will not only achieve sustained success, but you will also benefit from knowing that your hard work made it happen. And that hard work will come to serve you well when things go sideways or a failure comes into play. That resilience muscle is more important than you know.

One More Minute Rule

When it feels like you're failing at everything, give yourself one more minute to acknowledge that doing your best is enough.

7

Entrepreneurship:
Surviving The Potholes

I could write an entire book just on the jobs I had before the various breaks that led to my successful business. Those jobs helped shape me to the business owner I am today and were vital, each in their individual way, to solidify my resolve.

The following few were life lessons in disguise.

Ready To Work At Fourteen

My very first job was a cashier at a card store. I was so excited that prior to that first day of work, I went tanning and had fake nails put on so I'd look nice.

I hadn't realized that being a cashier at the store also meant blowing up balloons. One of my coworkers was showing me how, and I was so nervous I was shaking. She said, "Quit your shaking and get to work." And the manager felt so bad. She bought me a box of chocolates the next day as an apology.

Every job I've ever had, even when I was young, I was always the leader, and I didn't like working for other people. For example, I worked at a car wash as a cashier. I was making a lot of commissions, because you got money for upselling. Even then, I was working on how I spoke and related to customers.

One day, it was a poor weather day, and they were short-staffed, so I was also assigned to be the power washer. I sold a package to a guy that was a super-premium package that no one is ever able to sell. After the sale, the manager came up and deleted my name from the sales record and put in her name. I handed her the power washer, and I quit on the spot.

I worked in the reservations department of the Woodcliff Hotel. I liked chatting with people, and that job taught me customer service. One of my first restaurant jobs was at JoJo as a hostess when I was seventeen or eighteen. I remember I was overweight, and someone walked up to me and asked, "Oh, when are you due?"

And I was like, "No, I'm just seventeen. I'm just chubby." That was very deflating.

My first waitressing job was at a local chain restaurant—that was short-lived. A few months in, my mom had gotten in an accident, and she was in the ICU. I told my manager that I had to leave: "My mom is in the ICU."

He said, "Well, you can't leave until you dust all the paintings in the dining room." Can anyone guess whether I dusted the paintings? I quit. Don't disrespect my mother.

Even at a young age, I was clear on my worth, and when someone either didn't recognize it or tried to take advantage of it, I stood up for myself. I knew my worth, I knew someone else would want to hire me, and believe me, it would have been easy to just roll over and take the abuse from others. However, my mom stood up for herself in difficult situations, and I knew that took courage. I made sure I was clear on my value and made that value clear to others.

Sometimes The Potholes Are Caused By You

In my final semester of college, I secured a job earning $40,000 per year at a call center. I was selling internet, dish satellite TV, and home phone plans.

I still cannot believe this happened, but I dropped out of college (*failing out*) with literally weeks left of college. I would have gotten my associate's degree. I instead took this job. Even at an early age, everything I did, I strived to be the best. I ended up being one of the top five salespeople. A year later, I was offered a job to work from home because the company got bought out and everyone moved to Florida. I did not stay on because I realized I couldn't just sit at home. I was too young.

I knew I needed a trade to be able to fall back on if things didn't go well. And waitressing was not my trade of choice. So, I went to bartending school to learn how to be a bartender (which provides the opportunity for larger tips).

However, I did get a "break" when I became the personal assistant for the owner of a large company. She taught me quite a bit about business and life (shout-out to you, Dana, you are someone very important in my story, and you still don't realize it). I did some cooking, laundry, and errands. When she realized I was capable of so much more, she taught me how to manage her business. I became the general manager of her business. I handled bookkeeping, operations, and everything else.

The owners ended up getting a divorce, and unfortunately, with my position in their company, I was smack dab in the middle—meetings with attorneys, lots of stress. Nothing against the husband, but Dana was someone I really looked up to. I ended up quitting that job because it just became too stressful for me. However, I will never forget the lessons I learned during that time in my life.

Odd Jobs Do Not Define You

Because I needed to pay bills, and after endless applications, I ended up getting a job at a strip club. It was one weekend, but it was a horrible time. I was applying all over Rochester for a bartending job, and the only job I could get quickly was a "shot girl"—walking around the bar selling shots. I was a size thirteen wearing a short dress and a garter to hold the money. I was extremely uncomfortable—this was completely out of character for me. However, I did whatever it took, and this was no exception.

I was walking around selling $2 shots. I saw a guy from high school, and he said to me, "You're so much better than this." I knew that I was—I did what had to be done to get money in. However, I never lost sight of the fact that this was temporary and didn't have to define me in a negative way. I looked at this as being someone who was stepping sideways to get to the next path.

In between, I would always put ads up online to get side bartending jobs (having a trade to fall back on had been a smart move). I've been a backyard bartender—I went to a party and bartended for a couple of hundred bucks. Taking the time to learn how to bartend allowed me to take on odd jobs as I was looking for my next big opportunity. Those bartender jobs did not always go according to plan. *And I never forgot my worth.*

I ended up landing a job as the opening bartender of a leading nightclub in Rochester. This was a really big deal for me as I completely lied about my experience to get the job. I had to perform, and I did.

Here's a fun story for you—during my time at the nightclub, I sought a second job and applied to two restaurants. I was offered positions at both, and I had to choose. I ended up choosing the one that was more flexible with my schedule, allowing me to double dip and keep my nightclub job. Unbeknownst to me, my now-husband was the opening pastry chef of the other restaurant. I would go and have dessert and wine there after my shifts, not knowing that his signature recipe was my favorite dessert.

I ended up getting fired from the restaurant job. To make a long story short, an entitled group of VIP customers came in and complained about me when they shouldn't have. I know I did nothing wrong, and honestly, so did management, because they couldn't fight my unemployment claim. At the time, I was upset, but I ended up being OK with them firing me. That paid for me to live during college. That is how I was able to afford going back to school, the bare minimum to survive. Unemployment benefits were a lifeline.

I was never afraid to take risks, even during periods of financial distress. I would take the risk for a job, knowing I could always exit and look for something else. There is always something else coming along—you just have to keep pursuing to get there. I knew my worth. I knew what I was capable of, and I knew cream always rises to the top (an expression my grandma would say constantly).

I've had plenty of other jobs, ranging from a bartending stint that lasted a whopping twenty-eight minutes before I quit due to lack of supplies and management, to the bartending job I lost because I was rude to someone outside of work who knew the owner (be careful how you interact with someone—you never know who they may know).

I've done it all, from babysitting to bartending to administrative work, to now being the CEO of a multimillion-dollar company.

The one job that I am the best at? Being Shaina. I know I will always succeed, no matter what, and I know my worth.

If you learn one thing from this chapter, it is to know your worth. Don't settle for less. You have one life, and if you don't always strive to make it what you want it to be, what is the point?

Sharing The Power Of Knowledge

I also share my knowledge with my community. I love to write. I wrote a column at my school on health, and I write for the local business journal. And this book is a culmination of my experiences and continues to be an incredible journey.

My best/worst quality is that I can't keep my knowledge to myself. I always share and always will. I won't keep my mouth shut when I see someone struggle. I show up and give more than expected without expecting anything in return. But if you're going to treat me like garbage, you don't deserve what I'm bringing to the table.

Applying The Shaina Rule

Never compromise on your value. How you allow people to treat you is how they will see your value. And sometimes, you have to walk away to keep your worth intact.

Every experience leads you closer to the success you want. It may not be evident at the time, but there is a life lesson in every situation.

One More Minute Rule

When failure hits, take one more minute to ask, "What is this teaching me?"—then rise again.

8

Success Is Never
A Straight Line

*I*t makes me a little crazy to hear other motivational speakers on stage. Not that I don't find their success an inspiration, but what gets me is that they talk about the last 5 percent of their journey and not the 95 percent of hard work that led up to it.

Sure, when you present the last 5 percent of anything, the odds of it being point A to point B are high. When have you seen someone in life simply decide they wanted a level of success, and they saw a clear path to it?

Success is not a straight line. A lot of times, influencers and executives only talk about where they are now. I have no problem telling people all the times that I've failed.

Success isn't just arriving at the top, unless you're some very lucky kid who inherited something. It's a struggle.

Seeing The Road For The Journey

A great example is my company. I love sharing the story about starting my company and the crazy journey I have been on.

I hit one of my milestones, and it felt like we were starting to be OK. We ended up getting a new kitchen. We started renovating the kitchen, and I was so excited. "Now we're going somewhere." Then, I ended up having quality issues with my product. I had spent all this money and time creating this amazing kitchen and moving my company out of my food truck, with just my mom and me as employees. And we suddenly had negative bank accounts. We had no money and no business, and now had to pay back a loan for the renovation and the rent on the space. I had to act and act fast to pull myself out of this.

We were the definition of screwed. I looked at my mom at that moment, and I said, "Mom, this is it. There's just no way we can keep going."

And she said, "We're too far in, so figure it out."

I had to figure out how to fix everything. I thought about everything, and I remembered all my connections at the hospital. I was really good at what I did at the hospital. People were trying to poach me when I worked there. People wanted Shaina.

That's the thing with business: They're buying you. They're not just buying your product. They don't know the company, so they really are buying the owner.

Well, I was sellable. They wanted me to stay at that hospital. So, I reached out to a top executive at the hospital who believed in me, and she ended up getting me on a preferred vendor list.

From that connection, I restarted my company, doing corporate lunch catering. My relationship with the hospital kept growing and growing. That prior journey at the hospital led me to my focus on healthy eating, and that led me back to my roots at the hospital. Those connections from my past helped me create my future.

The Curve In The Road Can Lead You In The Right Direction

I have shared how I have had one million setbacks, and I have committed to getting back in there one million and one times. Setback #22: I worked at and failed in my food truck, despite some initial success. Setback #38: I built up a solid customer base, only to see the quality decline and the customer base drop back to where I was in the first six months of working. Potential setback #19: I had to navigate a pandemic that could have made or broken my company for good.

My company started in 2013 as a meal prep company run out of a food truck. I got the food truck because I didn't know what I was doing. I had talked to many people who had me believe that having a food truck was the only way to go. I didn't know what I didn't know, and I trusted the emphatic advice of others. They said that the way to success was to run the meal prep from a food truck. That ended up being the wrong advice.

After this misstep, I started to run the meal prep out of my own kitchen. During this time, I made the decision to quit my full-time job because I couldn't do both.

At the end of 2014, I met my husband, Mike. At that time, I was renting a kitchen at the City of Rochester's Public Market, and an opportunity came across my path: gym clients. They had a client base already focused on fitness. It turns out that many of these clients wanted to add nutrition and diet to their health habits. I had to get onto social platforms to show my credibility and talent.

The power of that social media push helped me gain access to several gyms and tap into the clientele looking to buy meals prepped for cooking. I naively thought I could grow with little staff and resources. I was doing great, and then I got too big too fast. You could say I had horrible growing pains.

In May 2015, I moved into another professional kitchen. At this point, I had built up what I thought was a solid base of customers and thought renovating a new space would be the right move. During the construction, I thought I could save money and run the business out of a food truck.

I found out quickly that you cannot successfully run quality meal prep for a hundred or more customers out of a driveway. By the time construction was done, we had lost over 90 percent of our customers. All those people who had given me advice that having a food truck was the way to go ended up being completely wrong. But I suffered the consequences of taking that advice.

I had to get money in and was open to any pivot that would make that possible. I saw that Mike was doing well as a caterer. I had come from one of the largest hospitals in the area, and still had connections. So, I targeted hospitals, leveraging the relationships and the knowledge that I had. I knew, at the end of the day, that I needed to go back to basics: create a quality menu with good products and recipes.

I ended up hiring a woman who was great at sales, and she got my business moving again. I decided to lean into what the market needed and where my focus started: providing quality meals and quality service. This meant things like getting back into the car and driving back to return with the dressing that was missing.

I returned to the new-business-owner mindset and made sure whoever ordered my meals got exactly what they wanted, as if they were my first customer ever. In fact, I have returned to getting on the phone to chat with potential customers. Those customers love that I am answering the call. And just as importantly, I am excited when I get a sale.

Fast forward, and we ended up creating this multimillion-dollar company. And there have been so many times that I've been feeling super low and had many failures. It could be a small failure, like screwing up a catering order and forgetting to give the person a sandwich and now they're never going to order from me again. Or it could be a large failure, like having negative bank accounts.

It is the small wins that propel us forward. The other day, I made two sales totaling $200, and I said out loud, "This is the best day—I made this sale!" Let the small wins excite you.

However, it's important for people to know that it's very real to fail. What is important is what you do with failure, how you learn resilience, and that you don't give up. That will bring you to success.

Mrs. New York America/American Pageant— Crowning My Own Path

Mrs. New York wasn't just a pageant to me—it was an idea. A possibility. A bold move I decided to make when the traditional avenues to grow my motivational speaking platform weren't moving at the pace I wanted.

For years, I had been trying to find my way onto stages to share my story, my lessons, and my message. When I decided to accelerate this endeavor, I did what I've always done: I found another door. Or in this case, I built one.

I didn't grow up dreaming of a crown or pageantry. Truthfully, I don't love wearing makeup. Walking in heels? Not my thing. The idea of strutting across a stage in a gown and being "on" was terrifying. But I saw a bigger purpose.

I saw an opportunity to show women everywhere that we don't have to wait for permission. We don't have to fit in boxes. We can be both survivors and queens. We can reinvent ourselves at any time.

So, I stepped way outside of my comfort zone. I learned how to walk in platform heels. I practiced posture and stage presence. I leaned into glam. And I came to love what it represented: not vanity, but visibility.

Women like me, who came from hardship, who were overlooked, who were told they weren't enough, deserve to be seen.

This journey opened doors I never expected. I realized that the pageant's mission aligned so beautifully with my own. Their commitment to changing lives, uplifting women, and supporting Victoria's Voice Foundation—a cause deeply tied to my heart through the memory of my sister, Nikki—made it all feel right. It wasn't about winning a sash. It was about amplifying my purpose.

When I gave a speech to a room full of juniors and seniors, I told them the truth that I was bullied. I used to skip lunch to hide in the bathroom and do my makeup. Kids called me ugly and said that I looked like a boy. I watched my mother get hurt, emotionally and physically, and carry the weight of raising two daughters alone. I felt small and invisible. But I also told them how those moments were the seeds of resilience—the start of everything I've built.

Yes, Mrs. New York started as a creative way to grow my reach. But it morphed into something more: a way to honor the girl I used to be, the women I hope to reach, and the sister I lost. A way to wear resilience—not just on my sleeve, but in a crown. A way to remind every woman reading this that we can write our own chapters—and they can be bolder, louder, and more beautiful than we ever imagined.

After attending Nationals, I realized being a queen and the pageant world did not align with me. I am Shaina, an entrepreneur. I resigned from my title in August 2025.

Applying The Shaina Rule

When you feel like you are struggling, go back to the beginning. What was your brand's purpose? What activity made you proud at the end of the day? What small wins can be added to your "pat-on-the-back" file? Don't dismiss where you started and what success looked like at that time. The start of every journey begins with that first step, and each step is as critical as the previous one and the next one.

Look for new ways to express yourself, grow, and inspire others because your story matters at the end of the day.

One More Minute Rule

Every morning, take one more minute in the mirror to speak to yourself with power, not punishment.

9

Turn Every Setback Into A Comeback

homas Edison said that he hadn't failed. He just found ten thousand ways that won't work. And it is way number 10,001 that oftentimes gets you to your success point.

No one wants to fail. It is in our very DNA to keep ourselves safe. When we do fail, it feels horrible. Even if we have had successes up to this point, facing that failure can drain all our confidence and energy.

A Misstep Can Lead To An Unimagined Success Point

My husband, Mike, had a kitchen on East Avenue for his company, Chef's Catering. At that time, his company was growing too big and he needed to find a new space. He ended up finding a building that was up for sale that used to be the local deli.

Unfortunately, he didn't do his research properly. He purchased the building and put his catering company into it. There was a big parking lot, and there was enough space for his food trucks.

It was big enough for him to grow, and there were plans also to use the storefront as part of the expansion.

His first miscalculation was the parking lot. The parking lot didn't have paving. He spent tens of thousands of dollars paving the parking lot because he wanted to make a strong first impression for the company.

The second issue was that some locals in the town were dead set against having Chef's in this spot. In their minds, the traffic would destroy the ambiance of the small town. They saw a guy with ideas too big for their small community. That did not sit well with them.

Now, Mike was deeply invested in this place, at least $100,000, and he needed the kitchen to be completed for the catering side of the business. He went to countless town planning board meetings to try to get approval for the work. He retained attorneys to try to fight. Ultimately, he ended up losing the battle and forgoing all of his investments in that place. However, that turned out to be a blessing in disguise.

He remembered it was never his goal to have a storefront. He never wanted to be a deli. As luck would have it, a party house that was only three minutes around the corner from our house ended up going up for sale. Even though the first investment did not pan out, he took a leap of faith and bought that party house. And this time, he put himself into millions of dollars of debt to renovate the entire place, as it needed a complete gut job.

He essentially had to start over. Yet it ended up being a good start over, and in a way he could not have imagined. The party house removed the need for him to be an on-site wedding caterer everywhere to get business. He could still do on-site events, but it was no longer a requirement. This massive party house can accommodate 350 people inside, and it also features a stunning outdoor area, making it perfect for events.

This failure ended up making his dream become better than he imagined. He now has his own party house and event center that is close to our home, so he can run his business and be present for his family.

The misstep helped him find the right path, and the transformation for his business has been unbelievable. While I believe he would have been successful in that storefront, the sacrifice that would have been needed was not yet clear. We had just had our first child when the storefront was purchased. That pivot made a balance between home and work possible, and that balance was not something on our radar as new parents. The failure caused a change in focus and a better success story.

You Never Know When A Moment Will Be The Last One

The last night I saw my sister, Nikki, I had invited her to a Dave Matthews band cover band concert (Dave Matthews being one of my favorite bands). She hated Dave Matthews, and I thought for sure that she was going to say no to coming with me. She listened to gangster rap music, and Dave Matthews is the opposite of that.

She showed up for the concert. I remember that she was happy, smiling, and hanging out with my daughter, Zoe. We had dinner outside our friend's food truck. I can picture this as if it were yesterday. She was eating kebabs. My daughter was eating pizza, and they were sitting together outside of the food truck.

She then took videos of me dancing with Zoe, and the last picture I ever took of Nikki was of her holding Zoe. She was so happy, and then all of a sudden, she disappeared. I never saw her alive again.

Later that night, I texted her and asked, "Where'd you go?" She wrote me back and said, "I had a really bad stomach ache and I had to leave."

The Call That Never Came

I knew she was going to get mad at me the next day because she had taken my credit card and bought herself cheesy tots from Burger King the day before. Because of that, I kept $20 out of her paycheck. She worked for me sometimes. Some days, she was my hardest employee. Sometimes, she'd show up, and she really helped me. When we were broke and couldn't afford much, she gave us help. As wonderful as Nikki was, she also struggled with drug addiction. She was my best employee when she was there, and she was the worst employee when she would call out.

I held that money out of her paycheck, and I knew I was going to get a call that next morning saying, "Where's my $20? You kept the money!" In her mind, she didn't steal my credit card to get her cheesy tots. She just used it to get something, and that was no big deal. I never got the call. I knew something was wrong. My mom was in Pennsylvania at the time to say goodbye to my grandmother's friend, who was dying of brain cancer. I called her and said, "Mom, something's not right. Nikki's not answering."

She couldn't get a hold of Nikki either, so my husband went and tried to look through the windows. No one was answering the door. We couldn't get into the apartment because we didn't have a key. My mom told me, "I have a really bad feeling."

We got access to the apartment, and there was Nikki, lying dead in her bed. She had been five months clean at the time of her overdose. Fentanyl ended up getting the best of her.

The memory of the day we found my sister is something that I can see clearly even today. In addition to all that, we had to return to work because we were the primary employees. We couldn't take days off. We just kept going because there was nothing that we could do.

We lost Nikki. We couldn't bring her back, and we still had a company to manage. This is where you find out what you are made of, and this is the definition of being strong-minded.

Losing my sister made me realize how short life is. Instead of living in grief, I use it as fuel to create the life that I've always dreamed of, no matter what struggles end up in my way.

Nicole Helen Sidoti. 1989-2018

The Pep Talk (And Help) When I Needed It

My mom always says, "Your life is your choice." Everything you do is a choice.

There have been several times where I wanted just to throw in the towel and say "I am done." My mom would give me the right pep talk at that time. She just told me, "We have to keep going." The option is to choose to keep going.

I would've made more money selling bang bang shrimp than I was making in 2015. I didn't take compensation for three years. I had to write myself a paycheck for $333, just to pay myself something. I just never cashed those paychecks.

My mom did not make a penny. I now am able to give my mom the life she deserves and never see her struggle again. I am immensely grateful that she worked for me for so long. We worked like mad, harder than you could imagine. I reflect on all we went through and am still amazed that we were able to do what needed to be done.

On a particular day, my mom was grabbing a case of jarred red peppers when she fell back, slipped, and hurt her back. I then had no one else to help me. I honestly didn't have many friends at that point.

So, I called Mike. I had just recently met him. I didn't want to look like I didn't have everything together. But I really needed some help, and I had to be OK with asking for it.

He came and he stood in this kitchen chopping sweet potatoes with me, helping me for hours. He had his own company to run.

He was new in his business. He didn't even know me that well, but he helped me when I needed it. He ended up being my ride-or-die partner. Not all partners will drop everything and come to help you, especially when it is not convenient for them. When you find that ride-or-die partner, hold onto them. They are a gift.

Applying The Shaina Rule

Be OK with removing people from your life who do not have your back or are preventing you from moving forward. Life is hard enough as it is—having extra weight will only cause you to stumble.

Don't be ashamed of failing in public. You never know who will become your ally and be ready to step up and assist you. Asking for help is not a weakness but a strength. Because many hands make light work, and there are times when you need many hands.

If everything was easy, everyone would do it. Be OK with being uncomfortable.

One More Minute Rule

When you hear no, give yourself one more minute to find the new direction that no just revealed.

10

Celebrate The Progress, Not Just The Goal

*I*t is so easy to look at what we have not completed versus what we have. It is easy to forget what we have accomplished. I still have to take a step back and evaluate my life, all the things I have accomplished, and what has gotten me to this point. And it is easy to gloss over the wins under your belt.

It is critical to keep reminders of your success and track your accomplishments. If you can look back at your progress, it will fuel you more than if you focus on what you're lacking and what you don't have.

At the beginning of my journey, when it was hard, I would sometimes think of what I didn't have. But I'd always think of what movement I had made more than what I didn't have at the moment. Yes, my business shrank at one point, but I still had a few customers and I knew I could build things back up if I paid attention to why those customers stayed. I never thought that anything was out of reach. I knew some things were harder to get to than others, but not impossible.

When you start to get momentum, it can feel like things aren't progressing as quickly as you would like. This is when you should put all your positive intentions into it, which will help you take action.

I think that, whether in business or health, a really successful person always wants more. A truly successful person is never truly satisfied. I could have been satisfied with making this company a multimillion-dollar company. I've hit every goal. I've supported my mom and my employees. But now is the time to go to the next level, which is why I'm on chapter two of my life. My next goal is to inspire people because that's something that's always been in the back of my mind that I've wanted to do.

Only When You Are Ready

You have to do things when you're ready. And you have to wait until the time is right. Being patient is key. It's been my goal for years to be listed as one of the top 100 companies in Rochester. To be considered for that list, your company has to make a million dollars for three years in a row. It forces you to apply what you did to make a million dollars on repeat.

In 2019, I did it. And then 2020, I didn't. Instead of being angry in 2020 that I didn't make a million dollars, I reminded myself that I didn't go out of business.

My biggest thrill during the pandemic was giving back to my community. By creating a donation drive, people were able to donate and help provide meals for healthcare workers. This resulted in over $50,000 in box lunches sent out to those healthcare workers.

I could have focused on the negative. Instead, I realized I had to figure out a way to get through a pandemic. I pivoted. I believed in myself and my company, and did it with a newborn baby and despite the death of my grandma, who was one of the most important people to me.

Then I just kept looking forward and searching for what I could do next. It's all about your mind. It's about what you tell yourself you can do. If I didn't believe that I could do what I achieved, I wouldn't have achieved it.

You're only going to be as successful as you think. I have that 1 percent mindset, and that's why I keep succeeding. And worst-case scenario, if everything failed and I lost it all, I know I'd be OK, and I'd figure something else out. It comes down to being strong-minded.

Keeping That Voice Going

I love both of my grandparents, and my grandma has a very special place in my heart. My grandparents watched us quite a bit. My mom needed help. She was a single mom.

We spent a lot of time with Grandma. And it's funny to see the difference in grandparenting styles. My mom plays with my kids. My grandma would just sit there in her chair. We would just sit on the couch, but we would spend time together.

Grandma always taught me to keep my mind sharp. She would do all the crosswords every Sunday. She'd do the most challenging ones. And before Google, Grandma knew all the answers. My sister and I would always joke that if we were ever on a TV show and needed to phone a friend, we would call Grandma, and that's how we would win.

Grandma also taught me to always have my own money. You never share all of your money with a partner.

She also instilled the belief that you can do for yourself. She was an extreme feminist. I have a painting of hers that is a true definition of girl power. When I took a women's studies course in college, I brought the painting to school. They were so impressed by it that they wanted to keep it on campus.

Grandma taught me that a woman is just as powerful as a man. You can be anything you want. She taught me how to be brave because she was one of the most courageous women I have ever known.

When Grandma found out she was dying of cancer, she called all of her friends to tell them. She ended up comforting everyone else, and it was the most heroic thing I have ever seen. She was dying of stage four pancreatic cancer, and she wanted to make sure that everyone else was OK.

Her friends loved her so much that they held a parade for her during COVID-19. All of her friends made signs. She sat in the driveway of her house in her wheelchair, and everyone drove by holding signs. And one of them said, "Helen for President." That was her last week on this earth. Everyone showed her how much she was loved.

My grandma has her own monument right in front of the college, featuring her picture and showcasing her paintings. Donating was in her blood, as well as always wanting to do good for people. I joked that if I was in charge, she would've been rich selling her paintings. She would donate paintings that took her forty hours to create. She didn't care. She just wanted people to enjoy the art, and she didn't need a lot of things. She taught me to give back and is an influence in the scholarships I have created for young women.

Grandma wanted a modest, happy, comfortable, middle-class life. It was enough for her. But she would teach me to go on adventures. That's where I learned to take care of my kids and take them places. My mom didn't like going to museums. My grandparents did; they would take me to the Genesee Country

Village & Museum and the Corning Museum of Glass. Both of my grandparents, and my grandma especially, appreciated art. Because of my exposure to museums and to art, when I go to an event or a festival, I always make sure to buy something from a local artist.

Grandma was the real core of the family. And when she died, my whole family fell apart. Holidays were never the same. She was my best friend. She was the person I could tell anything to, and she never judged me. I think that's why I never wanted my grandma to know when I was failing. I knew she wouldn't judge me, but I wanted her to believe that I was something.

I still remember when I was able to tell her that I had $100,000 in the bank. I told her I was going to have a million dollars someday. And she was like, "I knew you would do it," and she knew I would turn it into a million.

When I saw that number in my bank account, I felt like I had made it, and Grandma was the first person I told. I knew she wouldn't try to take advantage of it. She wouldn't ask for anything. I knew she would just genuinely be proud of me.

Doing Things The Way They Should Be Done

My grandma was a very meticulous woman, too, and set in her ways. One time, she had me clean her house. She had me cleaning the windows. Every time she saw a streak on a window, she'd make me redo it.

She taught me the importance of hard work. One time, she had me wash the walls. She gave me a sponge with Dawn soap and water, and she made me wash her walls. I'm like, "Who washes a wall?" She taught me things that you would never think of learning. I now have it as an item for my staff to wash the kitchen walls and my home walls are always clean.

My grandma was a grandma in every sense of the word. She wore sweaters, had short hair, and wore glasses. If you think of an Italian grandma, that was her. She only had one person in her life whom she didn't like. And because she's such a good person, she didn't even tell them that she didn't like them.

My grandfather loves her so much. I remember one time we went to the movies with them, and I looked over and saw that they were holding hands. They were till death do us part.

My grandfather was more of an intellectual person—he had a PhD in philosophy and was an intelligence agent in the army. In college, I'd make sure Grandpa always proofread my papers. I would always report my grades to him. He liked seeing good grades. He was my go-to expert for proofreading in high school and college, and was always the person I could go to and present my work to. He would provide feedback and ensure that what I had created was excellent.

I'll never forget one time, I went to him crying. I got a B, and I cried. I felt like a failure. He's like, "Shaina, you can't always be perfect." That was a good lesson to learn. Through his guidance, he instilled in me a love for education and taught me the importance of lifelong learning.

We spent so much time with Grandma and Grandpa throughout our lives. I still talk to Grandpa all the time—and I'm his barber. Ever since the COVID-19 pandemic, he has been afraid to go to the barbershop. I had to watch YouTube, buy clippers, and learn how to cut hair. So, I have one client in my barbershop business, and it's him.

He instilled many of the family values and beliefs that I now teach my children, including the importance of keeping traditions alive. I am so thankful for all he taught me. He is still alive at ninety-four, and I am so blessed that I can share my accomplishments with him. It brings a true joy to his heart and mine.

Recognize The Turning Point To Keep Going

I have seen my business pivot each day and even when I didn't hit the exact milestone at the exact time, I felt in my soul that I was on the right track. You will feel that turning point as well.

It is like a puzzle piece that you are trying to get to fit, and when you turn it the right way and it clicks in, the picture becomes clear. The object of the game is that when you hit that turning point, you don't let down your guard. The energy and resilience that got you here must continue. Believe in yourself, keep your focus and stay consistent. Keep steady, keep working, keep going —keep your fire. It is better to be a little uncomfortable and not give up or give in.

Each day is a day to either gain ground or lose it. Which will you choose each morning you wake up?

Applying The Shaina Rule

You don't have to be perfect. You just have to try and keep going.

Timing is not always what you think it will be. It is oftentimes way slower than you would like. That is the universe preparing you for what's next. Don't rush that training.

It is natural to want to throttle back when you feel the momentum growing toward your goal. That is when you need to lean in and push forward.

Nothing worth having will come easily.

One More Minute Rule

In the chase for more, spend one more minute being proud of how far you've already come.

11

Perfectly Imperfect

*Y*ou would think that the big setbacks are the ones that will knock you off your path and your game. Not true. The hardest hurdles to overcome are the small stalls on the road to success.

I want you to think of a great success in your life. I know you have one. If you didn't, you wouldn't want to reignite the fire within you. Now, take that success point and multiply it tenfold. That should amount to an incredible win!

On the road to that great success in your life, there probably was a small trip up or stall, but in that instance, it didn't derail your progress. That is because the delta gain between the stall and the success point was not a vast amount. Take your failure as a learning experience to grow and do better the next time.

And even when you have climbed much higher, and have a slight misstep, you may look back and be worried about how much more you have to lose. Keep that mental effort and keep going. The best way to go is up.

A Ten Year Courtship

I got married to Mike in 2023.

We had never felt the need to get married because we were happy with the way the relationship had evolved. And I had never known if I really wanted to get married. I wasn't sure if I wanted to change my last name or if it would be OK to do so. I never knew if I could commit to somebody like that. That's a big commitment to say, "I'm going to be with you forever."

Mike never said, "Shaina, just come and be part of my catering company." He lets me be fiercely independent.

I joke that he is my handyman. If I need something, he'll help me. He'll help fix anything. He's connected to me. But we always kept our businesses 100 percent separate, and that was always important to both of us. He worked very hard for his company and started it a year before mine.

I had a playlist of love songs I played in the background when he helped me, hoping that our day of chopping sweet potatoes together would make him fall in love with me. And "Fall" by Justin Bieber was on repeat that day—hilarious.

I don't feel that I am entitled to any of the business that he created for himself. And he doesn't feel that he's entitled to any of mine. That works for us. As I mentioned, my grandmother always taught me to have my own money. She had a secret bank account that my grandpa didn't know about.

The Perfect Time Is Never On Your Schedule

One day, Mike and I went to a five-star resort in New Paltz, New York. It's tremendous—a Victorian castle resort. Our daughter is maybe a year or two old. We go for a hike to the top of this mountain area. I have no idea why, but I start thinking he's going to propose. Now's the time. He is looking around and says, "Hey, you can see three states."

And I am thinking, "All right, where's the ring?"

He bends down to tie his shoe, and then he says, "All right, let's walk down."

I am like, "Are you kidding me?" I am so mad that I walked five feet in front of him.

I am so pissed. I keep thinking, "That was the time."

When it happened, it was 2017, and I will never forget that day. We went home and, from there, we were planning on going shopping. We were with his mom, his sister, and our daughter.

It was just a regular shopping outing. And his sister at the checkout bought these Mr. and Mrs. Coffee mugs. I remember seeing it and thinking, "Why is she buying those? Oh, maybe she's buying a gift for someone else." Then his mom said, "We have to go get that gift certificate, and I don't know where it is. Can I follow you there?"

So, we were driving, and I was starting to get annoyed. I was like, "Where the hell are we going? What is going on? Does your mom really have to follow us?" We pulled up at Water Street Music

Hall, which was where we had met when we had our food trucks. He parked in the same spot where the food trucks were. And this was on November 17—the date of our first meeting.

He got out of the car, and he was acting weird. And I was like, "What is he doing?" I was also worried and thinking, "Did I just piss him off so much that he now has to de-stress?"

And he opened the door, and he was shaking. He got down on one knee and proposed.

He had taken me to the same place where we met, which was really sweet. That night, I remember my sister was there; we were so happy. All of our friends came over. We celebrated. And then that night, something happened with my sister, and it had to do with her need to get drugs.

That's how it always was. Every time something was good, it was always crushed either by business difficulties or family issues.

In 2018, a couple of months before Nikki died, our kitchen was still located on South Avenue, and we were starting to get busy with catering. We had essentially grown out of there. My lease was coming up for renewal. I was aware that I wasn't this huge multimillion-dollar company yet. But I was making a consistent amount of money.

I had said, "We have to find a bigger place." Well, I'm getting nervous because now it's time. Our lease is up, and I have to figure this out. I'm either going to renew my lease or find somewhere else, but it's very hard to find a commercial kitchen for rent.

Through some connections, I found a place on Scottsville Road. Some people had wanted to make it a pub, and they had failed. An acquaintance of mine had bought the building. He renovated it. It was a mediocre renovation job, but it was enough. And, most importantly, it was an available commercial kitchen at a reasonable price. I could move in in two months. Mike said, "Go for it. You need it." So, I moved my company to this new space.

Our business was growing. We were now at the point where we had a couple hundred regular customers and were doing fifteen catering jobs a day. We had become a specialized lunch caterer to the point where we were overwhelmed. I had a full-time catering sales rep, and all she did all day was take catering orders. It was phenomenal.

It was also one of the best years in our food truck business. And then in 2019, we had another good year.

Almost Getting To The Top 100

To be considered for the top 100 companies list in Rochester, you have to make over a million dollars a year in revenue for three years in a row. In 2019, I was like, "Oh my God, two more years and I'm going to get that top one hundred!"

And then the pandemic happened. I remember we made just $850,000 in revenue in 2020.

It was a loss for me, and it sucked. Federal PPP loans were there, and that helped a little. There was a restaurant revitalization fund for which I was eligible, but unfortunately, too many businesses applied. My husband received his restaurant revitalization funds. I never got mine.

But I kept going. And in that same year, I received an email stating that we had been awarded a grant. The grant provided us with the opportunity to become the preferred meal delivery service for the University of Rochester Medical Center. The medical center would offer its employees a 25 percent discount, and we would bill the medical center that discounted amount. That's when it started—that's when I really started to gain a lot of business. I got a couple of hundred customers from that.

Starting from 2020, my company doubled in revenue and kept doubling again. I am now consistently making seven figures per year.

This road was not a straight line, but I got to the top. My success has never come exactly how or when I expected it to happen. And the smaller setbacks could have blown out the fire inside of me. Yet, I believe these smaller failures paved the road for even stronger success. In 2024, I made the list: #62! In 2024, my company was also named the #8 fastest growing MWBE in Rochester and #12 in 2025, as well as receiving an Elevating Women Award in 2025.

Applying The Shaina Rule

Even with opportunities, you cannot say "yes" to everything. Some things can cause you anxiety or stress, and the benefits may not outweigh those. If stress doesn't move the needle of success in a tangible way, is it worth your physical or mental health?

One More Minute Rule

When the road gets tough, give yourself one more minute to remember—this is how resilience is built.

12

Own Your Resilient Future

*H*ere's the thing: You can't control everything. There are a lot of unknowns. No one could have predicted that in 2020, we would have a pandemic, the world would shut down, and nothing would be the same.

What you can control is yourself and your goals.

Personally, I always have goals that I'm trying to reach. I want to be a good mom. I want to be a good wife. I want to stay as healthy as possible for as long as I possibly can. And I want to keep being successful.

I put it out there to myself, to the universe, to anyone who will hear it. I want to do these things. I will do these things, and I will continue to push forward. No matter what, I will continue to strive forward, and it starts with what's in my mind.

I know my future is going to continue to be bright, and I know that if I start to sink and the roller coaster goes downhill, I will always figure out a way to pick it back up. That's because I can't imagine anything being as bad as it has been in the past. I lost my sister. I almost lost my company a million times. All the things that I perceive to be absolutely horrible have already happened, and I am still here.

I like to think that my future's just going to keep going up. And I truly believe that humans have unlimited potential. I think that you can live and do whatever you want, and it starts with believing in the fact that you can do it.

If you want to be a bodybuilder, be a bodybuilder. If you want to be a millionaire, be a millionaire. If you want to get a new job, go for it. If you want to have another kid, have another kid. If you want to go on vacation, go on vacation.

It's up to you to start it. If you think you're never going on vacation, or you're never going to get a promotion, it won't happen. But if you believe you're going to get it, you're going to get it. And it's not the manifestation; it's not the genie. It's you. You are in control of your future and your life.

Getting Ready For What's Coming

You know what's fascinating about resilience? It's no longer about bouncing back—it's about bouncing forward. In today's world, with everything changing so rapidly, we need to completely reimagine what resilience means. Let me break this down in a way that really hits home, because this isn't just theory, this is about real life—your life—and how we can become stronger together.

The Mental Game

This is where your cognitive resilience training comes in, and let me tell you, it can be a lifeline. We've all been through stuff that felt impossible at the time. But just like you can train your body at the gym, you can train your mind to handle stress better. It's about building those mental muscles before you need them.

Think about it this way—when you're in the middle of a crisis, that's not the time to learn how to handle stress. That's like trying to learn how to swim when you're already in deep water. The time to build these skills is now, in the calm moments.

When my son was learning to ride a bike, he tried for two years to drop the training wheels. When he finally did it, he said to me, "Mommy, you just have to keep looking forward, not down or back." That is true for all things in life.

I'm not talking about just using meditation apps to manage stress, though they're great. It's about developing a comprehensive tool kit of techniques that help you stay strong when everything feels like it's falling apart.

However, here's the bottom line—all these tools and motivational speeches? They're just tools. The real power comes from you. It comes from believing in yourself and taking that first step. Because resilience isn't about never falling—it's about knowing you can get back up, no matter what.

Remember, every single person reading this has survived 100 percent of their worst days so far. That's not just luck—that's resilience. And with these new approaches I have described in this book, we're not just surviving anymore—we're learning how to thrive, no matter what life throws our way.

Think about it in a different way—every challenge you've faced, every obstacle you've overcome, has made you stronger. Now, you have the opportunity to build on that strength, creating not just individual resilience but collective resilience within your support group. Because when we come together, when we support each other, when we share our knowledge and our resources, that's when we truly become unstoppable.

Applying The Final Shaina Rule

If there is one thing I want you to take from this book, it is this: I believe you have the power to create a new reality for yourself. I believe this potential lives within you, dormant perhaps, but ready to be awakened through your choice and actions.

I want you to start to believe in that power and tap into it. I want you to recognize that this isn't wishful thinking but rather an acknowledgment of your inherent capacity to transform your circumstances.

Your life begins today, now, in this very moment—not tomorrow, not when conditions seem perfect, but in this exact slice of time where possibility resides. A good friend of my mom's used to write on my birthday cards, "Today is the first day of the rest of your life." I used to think that was so silly.

Now I understand.

I am right in the front row, cheering you on, excited to see what steps you will take toward the life you have always dreamed of having. I'm your biggest supporter, watching with anticipation as you break free from limitations that have held you back.

Yes, life will throw a bunch of curveballs at you, but you now have the tools to use your failures to create success. These challenges aren't obstacles but opportunities disguised as setbacks—each one offering valuable lessons that strengthen your resilience. You now know that anyone you admire had to walk through mud to get to their success point. Every icon, every mentor, every person who appears to have it all figured out has navigated their own swamp of difficulties and disappointments.

They may not talk about it, but that walk made them who they are today. Their struggles weren't separate from their achievements but integral to them. And that is what this book should do: shine a light on all the setbacks that have gotten you to this point. The difficulties you face are precisely what will shape your character and forge your determination.

Some days, you may only get mud on your shoes. Other days, you will fall face-first into it. But remember this truth that sustains through all circumstances: the mud will wash off. Your setbacks are temporary, but the wisdom they provide is permanent.

Now go out there and get absolutely dirty. Embrace the messiness of growth, the unpredictability of change, and the beautiful chaos of stepping into your greatness.

One More Minute Rule

When life breaks you, take one more minute to choose healing over hardening. That's where the growth begins.

Appendix A

Acknowledgments

When I first decided to write a book, I spoke with a publisher who told me that my story wasn't special, that it was ordinary.

I'm glad I didn't listen.

My story is important, and it is powerful. It is the ultimate story of resilience. I will never again be that kid who came home every day from being bullied. I will never again be that girl who felt left out, I will never be who I was in the past. But I will always have the past to help me remember and continue to be humble and resilient in my future.

I will continue to use my past to guide me into positivity and hope. I will guide my children with hopes for them to live their best lives, and will continue to use my experiences to help as many people as possible along the way.

To my mom, my rock, you win the award for best mom in the world. Thank you for everything you've ever done for me—it means more than you know.

To my sister Nikki, I miss you. I know you are proud of me. I just wish you lived to see what my life turned out to be.

To Grandma, my best friend, without you, I truly would not be who I am today. To Grandpa, you stepped in and gave me a fatherly figure when I didn't have one, and for that, I am forever grateful. I love you both.

To Mike, no matter what, together forever. I know our life has a lot in store for us, and I am really ready for the wild ride.

To Zoe, you were born a star, and someday you will have to take over for your mommy. You are the only person in the world whom I would trust, and I know you will shine brighter than a diamond. You are smart. You are beautiful. You are powerful. Never lose that. Keep being you. You are capable of big things, my girl. I love you.

To Michael, my sweet boy, thank you for making me take breaks to play with you. Thank you for being so innocent and sweet. Mommy needs your love just as much as you need mine. You're going to grow up to be the sweetest boy in the world. You are funny, you are smart, you are wonderful, and as you always say, "You are responsible."

To Alex and Nat, don't worry, I didn't forget you. Effortlessly Healthy would be nothing without you. I'd be nothing without you. You two are my rocks. Yin and yang.

To the rest of my friends and family, I cannot list you all. But you know I love you and am blessed to have your continuous support.

To Lisa, thank you for helping me find my true story—your coaching and expertise have been paramount for my success.

To my Zazzaro and Sidoti family, especially my niece and nephews, I hope your aunt inspires you to achieve all of your dreams. I love you all.

To my in-laws, I love you.

Appendix B

Big Four Shainaisms

1 It's not why, but why not?

---

2 You can have anything you want.
The first step is to believe, starting
with yourself.

---

3 Find your inner queen (or king).

---

4 You can manifest all you want.
It is up to you to make your dreams
a reality.

Appendix C

About The Author

Shaina Zazzaro, is a devoted mother, successful entrepreneur, keynote speaker, and author. As the founder and CEO of Effortlessly Healthy, she has transformed her passion for wellness into a multimillion-dollar meal delivery, wholesale, catering, and food truck company, recently named one of the *Top 100 Companies* by the Greater Rochester Chamber of Commerce and one of the region's fastest-growing certified MWBEs.

Shaina partners with organizations and audiences nationwide to teach one powerful principle: failure isn't the end—it's the beginning of a breakthrough. Drawing from personal experience, she shares how she's turned health struggles, career setbacks, and even moments of homelessness and near-bankruptcy into the foundation of her greatest successes.

Health is her passion, and she shares it boldly with the world. Shaina has lost over fifty pounds not once, but three times—twice after having children—and at thirty-seven, she's in the best shape of her life. Her journey proves that lasting change doesn't come from shortcuts, but from consistency, confidence, and belief in yourself.

Shaina is the creator of *The One More Minute Rule*, a powerful mindset shift that encourages people to give just one more minute of effort, even when it's hard. That one extra minute builds discipline, drives momentum, and ultimately leads to transformation.

Through every speech, she encourages others to stop fearing failure and start using it as fuel. Her signature philosophy is simple yet powerful: *Anything is achievable—if you start by believing in yourself.*

Known as *America's Breakthrough Success Coach*, Shaina inspires people to reclaim their health, rewrite their story, and rise into the life they were meant to live.

To learn more about her mission or to
start your own health journey, visit **ehmeals.com**.

To book Shaina or inquire about coaching,
visit **ShainaZazzaro.com**.

Follow her on Instagram @shainazazzaro
for inspirational videos!

Appendix D

Works Cited And Author's Notes

1   Rhonda Byrne, *The Secret* (Atria Books, 2006).

2   MyFitnessPal, https://www.myfitnesspal.com/.

www.ingramcontent.com/pod-product-compliance
Lightning Source LLC
Chambersburg PA
CBHW071709210326
41597CB00017B/2407